Unleashing Satan's Grip

Psychological & Spiritual Healing

ANNELIESE WIDMAN, PhD

authorHOUSE®

AuthorHouse™
1663 Liberty Drive, Suite 200
Bloomington, IN 47403
www.authorhouse.com
Phone: 1-800-839-8640

First published by AuthorHouse 5/1/2009

ISBN: 978-1-4389-6607-6 (e)
ISBN: 978-1-4389-6605-2 (sc)
ISBN: 978-1-4389-6606-9 (hc)

Printed in the United States of America
Bloomington, Indiana

This book is printed on acid-free paper.

Also by Anneliese Widman, PhD:

My Female, My Male, My Self and God: A Modern Woman in Search of Her Soul

Rage at God: Ascending to Reunion

Aquarian Amazon

When Spirit Takes Over

www.shortcuttogodself.com

Contents

ACKNOWLEDGMENTS

Two editors, one as different from the other as the night is from the day. Do I need two editors? I questioned myself, especially when I had to pay their bills.

I do. They are like branches from the same tree. We became intertwined and could not do without the other. We were three, like the Trinity. And like the Trinity, we had the same goal: truth said beautifully, honestly, meaningfully, all in alliance with our deepest inner voices.

Thank you, Elianne Obadia and Netty Kahan, for everything you offered in the time it took to bring this work to fruition.

Michael Grossman—a former patient, now a friend and champion of my work. Thank you, Michael. Your help will be memorable.

Fred Harris—designer of the cover of this book. You are so creative, so "with it," so unique. Thank you for your product.

PREFACE

Abraham Lincoln was known to have
prowled the corridors of the White
House at night, pleading to God for
direction for a nation in mortal
struggle. He went on record as saying,
"I should be the veriest shallow and
conceited blockhead...if I should
hope to get along without the wisdom
that comes from God and not from
man.[1]

Innately, though almost unconsciously, we all aspire to hear the
voice of God, to be counseled by God's wisdom, to have such a
presence flow through our natures every moment of the day. It is when
humankind surrenders to the credo, Thy Will be done, not mine alone,
that this experience of connection with the Divine never leaves us. But
the journey only begins when we ask, "Who am I, God? Who am I,
really—really, really?" It is then that the search for a larger concept of
living unfolds, until one day we can declare, like Jesus and many other
prophets and teachers did—"My Father and I are one." And when we
are one, we are filled with joy, love, wisdom, and wholeness.

Yet, through many years of working as a psychotherapist, I have
learned that some human beings choose to live their lives without
questioning or probing, much less seeking the Will of God or their
own true self. Instead, they are resigned (or sometimes even content) to
remain bound by their emotional handicaps: their physical armoring,
emotional repression, and spiritual blockages. These people remain

dead to their denial and lies, living like ants, carrying their nugget of materiality to their tribal dens. They close their eyes to rest (if that is what ants do), to awaken and repeat the same feat the approaching day.

But even when we have the willingness to look at ourselves, and a desire for oneness with God, it is not easy to find that connection. None of us on this earth is devoid of baggage that we carry with us into this life; therefore listening to the voice of God is a rarity. Why? Because the baggage creates a roadblock; we get detoured, choosing the left-handed path, the wrong path—accustoming our psyches to partner our lostness instead of persistently engaging our stamina and conviction to climb up farther on the rungs of the ladder to ascension and to the godly voices.

When we stray too long and too far, we become lost in an unlit labyrinth—hating ourselves, hating others, hating God, and hating life. We begin to listen to the alternate voice—the voice of a force that is so evil that it seeks to destroy us. Listening to that voice drives us to an even deeper estrangement from our real Self, the Self aligned with the Source, the Self that enables us to keep our feet on the ground and our hand always, *always,* reaching for God's.

I used to think that psychotherapy explained and cured all ills. All of my professional life, I refuted the concept of Satan. I discovered that I was wrong. I know now that Satan does exist and that its evil permeates us as a force outside of our own psyches. It is ever ready to infiltrate, unless we become aware of and are vigilant about our denials and vulnerabilities.

Twenty years ago, the topic of Satan emerged for me while I was avidly searching for a subject for my doctoral thesis. The following words appeared on a piece of paper one day as though I were writing them automatically: *The demonic aspect in the human personality.*

I was astonished, but I perceived the words and the concept underlying those words as manna from heaven; I realized that I was in touch with a monumental topic. I became aware that our insufficient egos stem not only from our parents' words and behavior, but also from the demonic *intention* that underlies the parents' feelings toward their offspring. I began to understand the ways in which the self could be destroyed by these voices, making normal functioning stilted and limited. I devised a construct, a method, to help identify these voices and help a patient extricate him or herself from the power of their irrational impact on the psyche.

As the voices were rooted out, a self emerged from the quagmire that was free of the infiltration. I am reminded of one of my patient's comments after she had applied the parental demonic method to her psyche and broken through to a self that had heretofore remained unavailable to her. She said:

> When the voices dominate,
> I feel anxious and depressed.
> But now that I can identify these
> feelings stemming from the voice
> of my mother, I'm no longer at its
> mercy. I can fight the voice and
> become me—not who my hateful
> mother told me I was.

I was delighted at the results and felt that I was being effective in the challenging field of psychotherapy. After repeatedly working with this construct and continuing to obtain noteworthy results, I thought that I had come to the end of this subject. I was wrong.

One Sunday morning, I was at a service in a Christian church. The Holy Spirit—a supernatural energy that is part of God—also known as the Paraclete, the Comforter, and by other names—entered my body and psyche. A foul-smelling, thick, black energy emerged. I was dumbfounded, never having had such an experience. The overseeing pastor whispered into my ear that the Holy Spirit was cleansing me and healing me. I felt as though a dark entity had been loosed from my body and psyche.

When I inquired of that darkness what it was, it said, "I'm your other self. I've been with you forever."

When I asked again what it wanted from me, it replied:

I want to possess you, make
you mine—
not God's, mine.

"Wow!" I exclaimed and fainted, slain by the Holy Spirit's energy.

When I came out of the swoon, I realized that I had heard the voice of Satan. Satan exists! And I, the psychotherapist, the therapized one, have this creature in residence in my body and psyche. This can't be. But its voice—cackling, smug, know-it-all—was real. I had heard it with my ears. I had sensed it with my body. It was in my energy field. It was like a wasp that had found its victim and was waiting for the right time to sting. And the sting, I surmised, would have an ineffaceable effect.

Contrary to what I had ever believed or imagined, I had experienced for myself that Satan exists, that it has a voice, and can invade a person's body, mind, and spirit. It has one intention—total possession.

Thus the concept of Satan emerged; taking me beyond the parental demonic construct I had devised to eliminate the destructive parental demonic voices. I now had to face with all my ingenuity, fearlessness, and skill what I had encountered in that church. The battle against Satan had begun.

I tackled this force in my own psyche before I was skilled enough to apply my discoveries to those in my practice. It remains the focus in my work—for the deeper we probe, the more likely that another encrusted, buried piece will be liberated from the rubble of Satan's destructive impact and added to the puzzle of who we really are, making us whole.

The process can take many years to accomplish. It comprises the content of this book.

It is a mammoth undertaking to find the true Self. The task is a noble one. But are we all not only noble but also godlike at our basic core? Is not the purpose of being on this planet to bring that core into the light, out of the unlit labyrinth, to completion—our connection to our Godself? I believe it is, and this book will demonstrate how to approach such completion, how to rid ourselves of a satanically riddled psyche. It is a way, perhaps a Way. Little or big, these ways have benefited me as well as the people I teach.

I often read books that show me clearer paths to living life. I feel saddened when I finish the last sentence of a powerfully illuminating book. My gratitude is boundless for what I had learned from the author.

I hope that *Unleashing Satan's Grip* will illuminate your life, giving birth to a Self that helps you walk hand in hand with the Source.

INTRODUCTION

We have been therapized, and therapy has become a way of life; in fact, for many it has become the Way. At social gatherings, we listen to others' conversations and recognize the psychoanalytic jargon. We feel safe around this jargon. Do we not mouth the same?

The Way after therapy? By then, we have a self, a little one, but we are looking for a larger one—a Self that will make our heart and soul quiver with delight and satisfaction. The little self struggles to grow into values that come not from our therapized jargon, but out of the chinks in our heart and soul that therapy has opened, so that the imprisoned splendor can be released drop by drop to wholeness.

Wholeness…a magical word; we all desire to have it, but it must be earned. And since we have undone a painful, tangled past through therapy, why not go further—all the way to completion.

Go all the way—engage the battle between good and evil, between God and Satan. But the psychological world has shoved this topic aside, relegating it to the occult, the paranormal, or to schizophrenia or some other insanity. We must therefore have the courage to open ourselves to new possibilities of exploring the psyche—beyond the usual therapeutic modes and the current model of parental abuse.

Little do we realize that our psyches are like Swiss cheeses that smell good and taste good but contain holes, breaks in our continuity that make wholeness seem impossible. Evil spirits pervade these gaps, but we are unaware. We do not become aware until they strike. These spirits manifest in the brain and in the body as voices, as negative energy, as irrational violence, as momentary or prolonged insanity, as unconsciousness without respite, as malice, depression without causes, distortions beyond belief, as worthlessness, as a multitude of neuroses and psychoses. The list could continue. Unless we recognize that the diabolic force is a treacherous deterrent to our wholeness, the diabolic will keep cozying up to us in the holes of our Swiss cheese natures.

Has it occurred to the reader that we as children are all drawn into that battle from the moment we are born and most likely before that? We have become tainted by our parents' shoulds and should nots, their indomitable superegos by which we are ruled. Frustration, terror, rage, and other hues and gradations of feelings govern our reactions to our parents' restrictive preachings. We become accustomed to listening to and rigidly functioning from those external ravings because otherwise our life might be snuffed out. Or, at the least, we might be sent into isolation.

Time passes. Childhood, adolescence, adulthood, old age come and go as the muddled ego continues to abide by the willful energy of those ever-chattering ungodly voices. The human being then slowly atrophies to become a shell of what he or she could have become.

"Ah!" says the person's core, located deep inside a *knowing self:* "I'm safe and have made it through life. It doesn't matter that I've become a mummy of myself, a hardly smiling, hardly tearful, hardly breathing, hardly living self. I've made it through life!"

And, having made it through life with little consciousness, with little introspection, with little respect for the godliness of our natures, we become rich fodder for the ravenous Satan, whose one desire is to contaminate God's creation through its infiltration.

The Not I, the I, and the I Am

In my practice, I have delineated the self as falling into three categories; the *Not I*, the *I*, and the *I Am*. (This category was devised at the beginning of the twentieth century by Yogi Ramacharaka. I believe he would be proud of my usage of it from a psychological perspective.)

The *Not I* is the state of lostness, misery, and unconsciousness created in the psyche of the child by parental abuse. It is known that this state can begin in intrauterine life, continuing through birth and throughout the organism's existence. Dr. Thomas Verney in his best seller, *The Secret Life of the Unborn Child*, gives ample scientific evidence that from the prenatal age of six months, the fetus reacts to the mother's emotional stimuli as well as to the environment. Hence there is recall from that period of time.

The *I* state is the ego development of the being that functions in the world: goes to school, pursues a vocation, enters into marriage, has children, and assumes a role in the world. Yet, as many have discovered, the day-to-day involvement with earth reality does not satisfy a yearning for deep connection, communion—with what, the *I* can hardly say.

The *I Am* state is our alignment to the whole Self, to God, the greater Self. It is our willingness to listen to the voice of God, by which we are directed and live. As I have written in my first book: *My Female, My Male, My Self and God: A Modern Woman in Search of her Soul*, in an *I Am* state,

> We are truth, we are love,
> we are joy, we are hope.
> We believe, we have faith,
> we know, that Thy Will
> being done, not mine alone,
> will bring us the right to our
> throne.[2]

Over time, it was revealed to me that the parental demonic voices are merely the tip of the iceberg. Beneath those voices, at the base of the iceberg, is the pervasive voice of Diablo. This foe stalks the weak, susceptible, wide-eyed human being until he or she becomes its prey. This instigator, this wielder of havoc creates disaster from one generation to the next. The parents of the abused child were infiltrated by *their* parents, and that generation was infiltrated by the preceding generation—all the way back to the Garden of Eden. Thus the voice of the Devil can be considered not only insidious but virtually eternal.

SATAN...DOWN THE AGES

Satan, Lucifer, Diablo, Devil, Azazel, Beliar, Belial, Samyaza, Prince of Darkness, Father of Lies—It is known by many names. Few acknowledge that It exists and invades us, even though two thousand years ago, an important aspect of Jesus' mission on Earth was to inform humanity that people are infiltrated and that the way to salvation is through him, his Truth and his Light. He said:

If I drive out demons by the power
of God, it is because the Kingdom
of God is come among you. It is
central to the war on Satan.[3]

The New Testament of the Holy Bible tells us that Jesus exorcized many demons from the souls of people during his three-year ministry, among them the soul of Mary Magdalene. When she was freed from the seven demons that had possessed her, she became her I Am and chose to follow the Anointed One to become one of his most devoted disciples.

In the Middle Ages, people possessed by demons were beaten violently to cast out the Devil, and if beatings were unsuccessful, they were immersed in water as in baptism. The methods employed were harsh and cruel. Because no one had the godly power to discern and cast out demons as Jesus had, the exorcee often was beaten to death or drowned. Ruled by dogma, the Church considered the exorcee an anathema to its goodness. Humanness was a nonexistent concept in the face of obedience to the rules of the often inhumane Church fathers.

As the psychological world emerged, other methods of casting out demons were explored. The most notable method was of Pierre Janet, a French hypnotherapist living in the early twentieth century. For example, he treated a patient named Achille, who was diagnosed as having demoniac possession. Janet duped the satanic energy within Achille by flattering the nature of the prideful demon. He then hypnotized his patient, who revealed the root cause of his disturbance: pathological guilt for his involvement in an adulterous relationship. When the cause of his pathology was discovered, Achille was forever freed from the demon's torturous possession of him. Through this unusual approach, it was recognized that the demonic could be perceived as a personality aberration—in this case, pathological guilt—through which the dark forces took possession.

During the twentieth century, four psychiatric geniuses appeared after Janet: Sigmund Freud (1856–1939), Wilhelm Reich (1897–1951), Carl G. Jung (1875–1961), and Alexander Lowen (1911–2008). All of them contributed to the understanding of the demonic from a psychological point of view. Both Freud and Reich refuted demonic possession; for them, the Devil did not exist. Freud believed that the Devil was a representation of base and evil impulses that had been rejected and repressed by the afflicted patient. When these impulses were uncovered and worked with, the patient no longer was a candidate for possession.

Reich believed that when the body is armored or muscularly contracted against *id* feelings—the source of instinctive energy—the person is projecting the body's sensations to the outside of itself to avoid the environment's dangerous condemnation and onslaught. He claimed that a rejected body externalizes its feelings into "voices" and imagery that could be likened to the Devil. He, too, believed that Satan was a delusion and that such a spirit would not be perceived by the patient if the body were unarmored.

Contrary to Freud and Reich, Jung did not entirely refute the actuality of possession by an external force. He believed, however, that the aim of one's life, psychologically speaking, should be to know one's other side, the shadow side (the repressed energy that stems from the personal unconscious). Instead of sublimating the shadow aspects as repressed, cast-off evil impulses of a person, as in Freud's beliefs, Jung ascribed power to the shadow force, feeling that it contains the seeds of a vital, repressed energy. The inferior, or dark, personality contains as much energy and potential as the superior. Jung was outstanding in his claim that all of humankind is divine in origin, and that knowing oneself and being true to that self led the way to a larger Self.

Most noteworthy among these giants is Alexander Lowen, who claimed that the demonic is the denial of an illusion that a person cannot bear to relinquish for fear of sinking into despair. When a person is desperately clinging to the remnants of an illusion—yet through the tattering fabric can see glimpses of the reality he or she has avoided throughout life—it is then that the demonic voice has power and the person might, for the protection he hopes it might provide, collude with the negative voice of the demon.

Lowen believes that the demon's voice is the voice of the rejected body taking revenge on the ego that denied the body. He also indicates that the demonic voice resides in the pit of the belly, just as Lucifer, God's fallen angel, took residence in the bowels of the earth._

These ideas are complex. My understanding is thus: When the person has no recourse but to face the *rock bottom* feelings of his or her psyche, that person, Job-like, enraged but desperate, screams out to the universe from indescribable anguish. And it is then that invasion happens. Invasion happens either by the Divinity or by Satan—depending upon the sincerity of one's plea. If one's fiber is weak, passive, without conviction, the person becomes susceptible to the ill-willed dark forces. If the psyche is of the fiber of a Job, Satan will be ineffective, as with Job.

To truly be transformed through our wrestling, our unraveling, we first must recognize that we are walking in an unlit labyrinth, a darkened maze, separated from our true Self, our *I Am*. We must recognize that we are infiltrated by Satan and its demonic cohorts. We must recognize that until we desire to be released from such incarceration, our intrinsic Self—our Godself—will be unavailable to us. Instead, we will participate consciously or unconsciously with the malevolent machinations of Satan.

When these realizations became clear to me, I—human being and psychotherapist—had little recourse but to go to battle with the dark forces. When I asked God for more understanding, the Divinity stated, "Satan and its demons are as plentiful as locusts in a drought period on your planet. My son came two thousand years ago to give you this message. You did not heed. Now that you have eyes to see and ears to hear, fight your fight. It will lead you to me and my realm."

It is not an easy battle to wage. And those people who have spent years "on the couch," so to speak, are weary warriors, insofar as satanic infiltration is yet another obstacle in the way of wholeness. This obstacle, however, can be defeated by our super-conscious efforts, and by a conscious self willingly allied with God. Such a union will render the dark forces helpless. We can master this foe through vigilance, determination, and warriorship for the *I Am*.

TOOLS FOR THE JOURNEY

To support you on your own journey from the *Not I* to the *I* to the *I Am*, this book was written on several levels—to engage your heart, your mind, *and* your spirit. In Part II, I illustrate the Bioenergetic tools as well as other methods I use for releasing the self from the insidious hold of the demonic. I also show how, even after the satanic hold is broken, unwanted patterns of behavior still lurk in the psyche when a person is indulgent and lazy in tackling this force. Free Will and forgiveness in alliance with God are scrutinized as well, revealing the role they play as necessary parts of the transformative process and expiation.

Without a story to make these tools come alive, however, this would be another how-to book. The best way to convey the gifts that have evolved out of my practice and my studies—gifts that were then reformed in the fires of faith and my own life journey—was to juxtapose and weave together story and exposition.

Over the course of contending with Satan and the parental demonic voices, I had the experience of the Holy Spirit laying out before me a story of two lost souls whom I call Gabrielle and Jesse. They are a composite of most of humanity: you the reader, my patients, and me. It is a tale that depicts two people whose *Not I-ness* attracts the satanic force to them. Their *I's* are undefined, reflecting the influence of Satan. Their *I Am* state is nonexistent and savagely denied, because they are listening to the voice of the Father of Lies.

As the recipient of this story, I had only to understand and work with what I was given. To do this I had to ask myself: Who and what is Satan? What does this evil force have to do with me and the method I devised many years ago? Why does it, unbeknownst to me, have a nest in my psyche? What is the meaning of the journeys of Gabrielle and Jesse?

Our passions, our actions, our struggles, our love, and our quest for knowledge and understanding are lived not merely linearly or rationally. To answer those questions, I realized I would need to employ my skills both as a psychotherapist and as a human being in touch with God's voice.

As the story begins, Gabrielle is sitting by a pond bemoaning her *Not I* state, when Satan, through its prowess, detects its prey. As a result, her life, as well as Jesse's, are about to change radically.

PART 1

THE STORY OF GABRIELLE, NATAS, AND JESSE

You can go crazy, your mind jibbering and jabbering: The neighbor wasn't too friendly today—was it something I did? The moon is full; the road will be brightly lit tonight. The television is too loud.

I ate too many sweets yesterday—my addiction, like my addiction to men. Always feel rotten when I indulge, whether they be sweets or men. I don't want to get fatter from sweets; I don't want to get diseased from men. But, I can't eat less food than I do, and I need the men's attention and l-o-v-e...or whatever you want to call what they give me. Maybe I should try to eat the right foods. I do, but I still get fat. Maybe I should wait for the right man—but I'd be so lonely. And besides, who'd want me anyway, with my questionable nature?

It's always about you, I continue talking to myself. Lift your consciousness. Okay, God. But God, where are *you*? Why aren't *you* talking to me instead of letting me froth at the mouth like a delusional human? Talk to me so I don't waste life, so I don't live from a rancid, rattling brain. I feel like Gabrielle, a strange woman—out of touch, in touch, conscious and that other word, yes, unconscious. Do you want me to say *lost*? That word scares me.

Lost—a void, a terrible *void*. I'm sitting on the grass, the goldenrod surrounding my naked body as I'm eyeing the pond. No one around but me—no man by my side. One big *blur*: The sky, cloudless, the hot sun, the water of the pond again. Moving in between the steady flow of the water are the bass or is it that the bass are moving in between the steady flow of the water of the pond? I'm not sure, not sure of anything.

One thought after another. I'll pounce on a thought like a mosquito and suck the blood out of it to feel alive. But the blood is dark and heavy and coagulating quickly. It dries before my sucking begins. Just let me have a tiny bit of nourishment, a dry speck of blood, I plead. It becomes a useless endeavor and the thought evaporates.

Wind, you bother me. Must you move so conspicuously? You're blowing away my papers, you're invading the emptiness in me, and emptiness feeds my victimization. Emptiness is a nothingness of its own, like—well, like nothingness, by contrast, victimization is warm, justifies my existence, a bubbly pleasantness. Don't disturb any of it. I don't want to chase my papers—I'm too tired, too angry, too frustrated. Everything makes me want to sleep. I do, but eventually I have to wake up. The foggy atmosphere of sleep lifts when I awaken, but the feelings are still hovering around like ancient obelisks, standing stiffly, noiselessly in the wind. Hah! You have feelings, though. I think silently. Feelings, yeah, a blob of negative, indefinable mush.

The branches crackle. A deer, I tell myself. They crackle louder and heavier. I look around and peer into the black forest. My attention is riveted to a figure sitting on a pile of rocks. "Who…*what*…are you?" I ask with a shudder, turning toward the apparition. "Are you real?"

It slowly becomes more visible. The figure is tall, growing even taller before my eyes to a length that reaches above the highest tree. And when it has reached its full height, it diminishes in size to that of a salamander with four legs and a long tail. The creature has a pink body punctuated by a fierce-looking crocodilian head and face, showing all of its dangerous teeth. I notice that when it turns sideways, its backside has wings that expand and contract as it changes its size.

"I'm real to some, but not to others," it replies.

"You look at me with a grin on your gigantic mouth."

"I'm glad to see you."

"Do you know me?"

"I know many like you."

I watch it move its jaws up and down repeatedly, then circularly—the teeth grinding hard against each other with a crunching sound. It swallows so forcefully that its body shakes from the effort while the saliva drools faintly from the sides of the jaws.

"You click your jaws as if you were already savoring the juicy meal I would become. Say something, Satan from hell," I scream from desperation. "If you've got something to say, then say it or leave!"

It hesitates, ceases the grinding of its many teeth until the jaws come to rest and a raspy voice emerges from two billowing nostrils that breathe out the next words:

"You call me Satan, but I prefer to be called Natas. This name is neither so common nor chastising, and I'm sensitive, you know. So, if we're going to get along, accommodate me.

I laugh.

4

"Laugh all you want," it says, waiting for me to have a better attitude. Natas does not budge from its position. Fear grips my insides, prompting me to look around for a way to escape. There is none, so I become femininely demure, knowing that any kind of aggression would be useless, perhaps fatal.

"That's better. Now let's go on. You're a beggar in life—without a visible begging bowl. Everyone feels your despair, loneliness, worthlessness. So, don't hide these feelings from yourself. Realize that they exist and let me show you how you've been living your life."

I'm aghast. How does this thing know my state? I wonder.

The creature is pleased by my reaction. "I'll tell you more," it continues, grinning: "You're part of a mob—the same as you, whom you refuse to identify with. But you are just like them. Don't fool yourself and think it's otherwise. One of the mob, a male, chooses to befriend you, squeezes your hand, invites you to a bar, and then to his home. No one greets you when you arrive there. You shrug your shoulders, thinking that you and he are alone. So you settle on his sofa, watch TV, drink a beer, laugh at the obscene, and sneer at everything that's different, anything that makes both of you uncomfortable.

"You're not alone any more. Doesn't that make you feel good, lost one? Why not have *another* beer? Beer makes it easier. Drink another and another.

"By now your host is slobbering on the sofa, groping for your breasts with one hand and your genitals with his other. He quickly removes his hands when the littlest of his four children enters the room. Startled by his son's appearance, the man kicks him in the buttocks. The poor kid scampers away, looking perplexed at his big father and the strange woman beside him. Hadn't his daddy played with him gently just that morning? And what were his hands doing to that lady?

"The child goes to the kitchen, but finds no joy there either. Mom, too, is slobbering. Too many drinks—red stuff in a coffee cup. The four-year-old wonders what is this that he's not allowed to have that she drinks from morning to night and then takes to bed as well. Mom pushes the perplexed child out of the way with a gesture of her right arm, like brushing crumbs off the table. He scampers outside and sits on a swing. His thumb, sucked to a fleshy, pointy appendage almost resembling an index finger, finds its familiar, perfect niche in his mouth.

Now he remembers a little of who he is. 'Mmmmm,' he murmurs softly to himself while his other hand finds the most delicate, soft strand of hair located at the top of his head. He caresses this tiny bundle of flimsiness, and through the thumb and the strand of fine hair he simulates a sense of comfort, of being wanted, of belonging.

"Then the call from the kitchen: 'Supper's ready.' It's accompanied by a heavy thud as the swinging kitchen door opens and the mother's body crashes to the floor.

"'It's okay,' says the host, staggering toward the kitchen. He picks Mom up from the floor, props her on a chair, her upper torso sprawling onto the table like a huge tarantula. All the while she gives her last command: 'Supper's ready.'

"You finally leave, unsteady on your feet. 'Thanks for everything,' you tell him. Neither of you has set a date to get together behind his wife's back. But never mind, that'll happen next time. He looks absentmindedly in your direction as you shut the front door.

"Outside, you think to yourself, it's not just me. You walk away to nowhere. Your steps are tentative—you're hoping to arrive somewhere, anywhere. It's not just me, you whisper to yourself, your jaw hardly moving. It's others, too. It's an epidemic—an epidemic.

"God, what is life all about? you wonder. It's so difficult! If I had a more artistic life, then maybe it would all be different. I'm so bored being a saleswoman in a department store. An artistic life would make me feel like something, somebody, someone."

The creature miraculously reads my thoughts and quietly stirs before me. It expands and contracts as it had done previously, becoming tall, medium-sized, small, and then repeating the unbelievable feat—tall, medium-sized, small. In this way it tries to get my attention. And it does. Its continuous body motion makes me dizzy. "Are you hypnotizing me?" I shout, ready for a battle.

"Look into my eyes," the creature says enticingly, ignoring my bravado. It faces me at the same height as I am. I jump back from it. Seeing my terror, it quickly reduces itself to the size of a salamander and walks steadily toward me.

"Don't be afraid. I'm small now, small enough for you to crush under your foot, if you so desire. Have the courage to look and listen and then you'll know more about yourself."

"I want to know," I convince myself, still terrified, but I gain more confidence as the salamander comes to my foot and rests upon it. It looks at me lovingly, pleadingly. I steady myself.

I'm challenged. The energy—a force that had heretofore been dead and unavailable—begins to rip through my body. I can't help myself. I look. The figure again expands to my size. Its two eyes merge, becoming one gigantic Cinerama, the screen three-dimensional, the sound track thunderous enough to deafen. But I look and I see, and I connect myself to something else beside me.

As I gaze into Natas' cinema-screen eyes, I see the figure of a man surrounded by a director, a producer, a film crew, and many others who participate in making a film. "This will be his fourth success," they all whisper among themselves.

The star is tired. This is a difficult one, he thinks to himself, seldom expressing his thoughts to others. I'll never do another film in an African jungle: too hot, biting insects, no respite from the "others," horrible accommodations—no accommodations—too far into the jungle to travel to a hotel. But I accepted the film because it will be a money maker. At this, he smiles and begins to hum a tune that he likes, composed for the film by somebody, what's-his-name—he can't remember.

⊷

He steps into a makeshift shower that has his name JESSE JASON printed on the shower curtain, which is draped around a gigantic showerhead. He scrubs his tall, bronzed, muscular, well-proportioned body vigorously, checking to make sure no ticks are lodged underneath his skin.

I'm somebody now, somebody, he thinks, smiling at his importance. At the same time he reaches out of the curtain for a towel. The attendant is a seventeen-year-old African crew member picked up from a nearby village to help the cast and appear in crowd scenes. He hands Jesse a large, blue, perfumed towel.

Jesse's eyes are waterlogged as he steps out of the shower and grabs the towel. He dries his body meticulously. When he has clearer vision, he notices the admiring eyes of the young boy and is impelled to strut around, perfecting the drying of his body, showing off his masculinity and his handsome face.

The attendant is awed by Jesse's blond wavy hair, his blue eyes that match the towel, and his strong body. He thinks that he would like to touch Jesse's hair—so soft, so light-colored—so different from his own. He imagines his hair to be like Jesse's. Would his sweetheart in his village like him better? What would she do to please him? She already does so much to make him happy. He wants to earn enough money to go to school. When he has graduated—but that's so far away —he'd like to have a good position, then marry his sweetheart, and have a big family. He sits lost in his own dream, his hands cupped around his cheeks, distant from Jesse's narcissistic strutting.

Jesse too comes out of his reverie, noticing that the boy is no longer focused on him. He makes a snorting, grunting, hissing sound that brings the young boy back to reality. The star, who had a few seconds ago been an idol to the boy, has turned into a monster with a huge, pink body topped by a crocodilian face, its jaws opening, ready to demolish him. The black youth backs away and flees in horror, his hands stretched out tautly before him to ward off the apparition.

Damn it all, curses Jesse. I shouldn't let this rage out without controlling it. How will I explain myself to the others? I don't have to, was his spontaneous answer. I'm Jesse Jason, the star, and I don't have to answer to anyone.

He turned his words to the parents he carried with him so vividly in his mind. I used to feel impotent, a real wimp with you, Mom and Pop, when I was a kid, a kid who'd wanted a new pair of shoes because the soles of the ones I was wearing had holes in them. Or a quarter for an ice cream cone. But you hollered at me so loudly, it brought the cops. Well, now I can buy anything I want and you don't get one cent from me for what you did to me.

He dresses himself quickly to offset the crowd of people running to his tent. "Are you okay, Jesse?" asks Frank, the out-of-breath producer. "The young extra came to us screaming that he'd seen you turn into a pink monster, ready to devour him. I wanted to make sure you're still alive."

Jesse assures him he's alive and well. "Maybe you should screen these extras before you hire them to make sure they're not chewing on a hallucinogenic bark."

"You might be right," replies Frank, "there's a lot of that going on in this area. I'll fire him—he's upset the entire cast and the star. Sorry, Jesse. It was a bad choice, but I can't be everywhere."

"Okay, okay," placates Jesse, "but don't ever let me see that kid around here again." He turns to the cast, "Now, why don't you all go back to your plush hotel rooms, have a drink, and get a good night's sleep?" he says with a good-natured chuckle. They all laugh at his irony and then scuffle back to their tents, relieved, arm-in-arm for safety and fellowship.

"He's a good guy with a sense of humor. This would have unnerved anyone," they comment to each other, "but he's got balance, a balanced guy, even though he's a celebrity."

Jesse too goes to his quarters: a tent with a cot, a mesh net suspended over it, a dresser, and a chair. The film company had given him a special African rug for the dirt floor next to his cot. Huh, sneers Jesse at their good-willed gesture. He stares at the meager contents of his quarters and wonders why he has subjected himself to such an ordeal. Three million bucks, he says to himself, and that's just the beginning.

He changes into his pajamas monogrammed with his initials, *JJ*. He remembers the times when he'd been ashamed of his name. He had changed it from Joshua to Jesse and his last name from Jacobs to Jason. Sounds better for the newspapers, he muses, looks better on the screen, and it has more appeal on the canopy of the theatres my films are playing in. *More appeal*—that's me!

He lies on his cot. If only I weren't so exhausted, he tells himself. I'm always exhausted. We did run the scenes over and over again, not because of me or the others, but because the animals weren't cooperating. Why can't I sleep? That damned kid. He almost did me in. Why did I ever promise to make a pact with the pink horror to listen to it exclusively—just to it and no one else? However, when I do listen to it, I get the breaks I need. And look at me now, I'm a celebrity. I've got everything—everything but the love of a woman. He is saddened by this last reminder to himself.

I'm good-looking, potent, and talented, but when there's a woman in my life and it looks serious, Natas shows up and takes possession of me, my heart, my life. The few women I was with saw what the African kid saw and they ran for their lives. How long can I do without love? How often do I have to prove to others that the apparition isn't me, and lie that it's the women's imaginations? I'm exhausted. I want to sleep.

"Natas, or whatever you want me to call you, don't come tonight—leave me alone, just for a night, please."

Just then, Jesse becomes aware of the salamander creeping up the side of his cot, lying seductively at the foot of it. Oh, no! cries Jesse silently. He doesn't dare object outwardly to the creature's presence, because past experiences taught him that rejection is a serious and dangerous threat to Natas.

He remembers all too well: At the beginning of their pact, Jesse denied Natas' wishes, and in a mere instant, he found himself dangling from a precariously perched tree off a mountain. At another time, when Jesse still was naïve and unbelieving of the creature's evil, he found himself swiftly and magically transported to a desert and buried alive in the hot sand. In both instances Jesse quickly learned to recognize who was the dominant power and relinquished his willful pride.

Remembering these events vividly, Jesse thinks, I'd better put up with him or I'll be dead. Maybe one day when I have all the money I need, I'll break our pact.

He looks at the salamander, which he's come to nickname Sal, and begs, "Please, Sal, stay small so that I can get one night of uninterrupted sleep." This compromise encourages Natas to sidle closer to him, its small salamandrine head resting on Jesse's thigh. Jesse turns away from it to his side and begins to sleep. As he snores heavily, the salamander's body heaves up and down.

The uncomfortable creature grinds its teeth, its desire for sleep thwarted. It enlarges its body and steals quietly alongside of Jesse's back, its now-monstrous head resting delicately above Jesse's head. And so they sleep peacefully until the first rays of the sun come into the tent. Neither of them has moved. Jesse, because his exhausted body desperately needs the rest, and the creature, because it wishes to show Jesse that it can be compliant.

Perhaps Jesse would not need the love of a woman if I were more loving to him, Natas reasons, and then our pact would become eternal and I will have gained another convert. With that new revelation, Natas smiles contentedly.

✍

Meanwhile, Kuwa, the young African, has been fired. With no salary, his dream of going to school collapses. He is frantic and knows without a doubt that he is not insane—he saw what he saw. His sweetheart and he conspire. They come up with a plan for him to go to the star's tent to apologize and to return Kuwa's job to him. She insists that Kuwa brave this task despite his intuition about an evil one in the tent. Kuwa agrees. After all, he rationalizes no star wants bad publicity. Kuwa feels powerful.

At the break of dawn, Kuwa quietly steals toward Jesse's sleeping quarters. He watches patiently from a distance for signs of stirring from the interior. He is familiar with the cast's routine: they rise early, exercise, conduct their ablutions, and then eat breakfast. Unfortunately for Kuwa the star is still snoring. I'll have to wait longer, muses Kuwa.

He is very alert, just as his sweetheart urged him to be. "This time there must be no mishaps," is her wise warning. So, Kuwa waits quietly, patiently. His eyes brighten because his "intelligence" notices that two snores are reverberating from the tent. He realizes that when one snore is inhaling, the other snore is exhaling—therefore two different people must be in there. Good logic, reasons Kuwa, "this will be an asset for school." And he pictures himself graduating with honors. How proud my sweetheart will be, he thinks, and he promptly forgets his caution.

By now, Kuwa's intelligence is hopelessly seduced by his fantasy of being an honor student. He does the unthinkable. He tiptoes to the entrance of Jesse's tent, eager to fulfill his mission, and he stares at the sight before him. At first his throat muscles grip. Now a spastic, choking grunt emerges as though he is trying to swallow saliva but can't. A more liberated scream follows the grunt, but not without great strain—finally, a blood-curdling scream shakes his body convulsively into all directions, mostly in circles. The words that scream forth are: *Rang-Ta! Rang-Ta! Rang-Ta.* Hyperventilating severely now, with whatever energy is left in his body, Kuwa pulls his dispersed breathing into the center of his being and dashes back to his village, continuing to bellow out those fatal yet mysterious words: *Rang-Ta.*

All who hear these words will remember them forever. They will remain emblazoned on their stupefied consciousness.

❧

Nor will Jesse ever forget those resounding words. Now alone in his tent—the creature has either disappeared or is hiding—Jesse springs from his cot. And once again Jesse sees the cast and all who are involved in the movie run to his tent.

"What's up?" Jesse screams at Frank, irate that this fiasco is happening again. "I told you to get rid of that kid," he roars at the producer.

"I did!" retorts Frank.

"Then what's he doing stalking me while I'm sleeping? What does he want? He's insane. Have him arrested."

"I can't do that. We'd have the entire community on our backs."

"This is infuriating. What are you going to do?" hollers Jesse. "We have one more scene to shoot. We're almost finished. Think of something quickly, or I quit. I can't take another episode like this, nor can the cast." With that he observes the frightened people standing around them, all in various states of emotional upheaval and physical undress.

Frank sputters to Jesse, "Let me sit down," and heads for the cot before Jesse can stop him. Jesse and Frank both notice a pink salamander sitting in the middle of it. When the salamander doesn't move, Frank brushes it off the cot. It hisses while reluctantly leaving its position. Frank remarks casually, "I didn't know that salamanders hiss. Do these creatures have wings?"

Jesse stands motionless in terror, praying that Lucifer—damn it, Natas—will behave itself and not jeopardize his career.

"Help me, Jesse," pleads the producer. "I can't think straight. There's one more scene to shoot and then we're out of here. I promise. What about the rest of you?" he asks, looking for advice from the cast.

"Let's finish," they agree in one chorus. "It's unlikely we'll be able to come back, and the financial backers probably won't support the expense, anyway. Besides, it's a good film and we don't want to forfeit what we've done." With this amount of unanimity, the place becomes peaceful again.

"Okay," says Frank, much relieved. "It's unanimous. Let's get to work. Go back to your quarters and be ready with makeup on, in costumes, in two hours."

Jesse heaves a sigh of relief. 'Saved once again, but for how long?' he thinks. He returns to his tent and looks around for the creature, but it's gone. Taking out his makeup, he looks across at his handsome face in the mirror on his dresser and thinks, Life is precarious. I've sold out, but it's better than being an upholsterer like my father, barely making a living.

Having decided to shower, he gets his blue towel and is about to take off his pajamas when the jungle suddenly becomes alive with people: men, women, children all holding blazing torches and chanting in unison, *Rang-Ta! Rang-Ta! Rang-Ta!* Their destination is Jesse's tent. Jesse's intuition tells him to run for his life. He spots his personal van filled with movie equipment and his wardrobe. At the same time, his driver dashes to the van.

All are motivated by the same purpose; and the jungle becomes a cacophony of the sounds of keys hurriedly stuck into ignitions, feet on gas pedals, the roaring of motors and then the whirring of wheels spinning and the clunking into and out of ditches, and the crackling of branches underneath the tires. Then, finally, they reach smoother roads and roads that lead to the nearest and largest city. Meanwhile, the villagers are left behind, shouting those enigmatic words while brandishing their lit torches in the direction of the disappearing vans.

Jesse's driver finally asks out loud: "What are they saying, Jesse? Do you know what those words mean?" Jesse says no with his head while his heart and mind are silently murmuring: *Devil.*

❧

The entire film company is on its way back to the United States after a few days in a luxurious hotel where they engage in their civilized activities, readying themselves for the long trip back to Los Angeles and the final stages of the film.

"What now, Frank?" Jesse asks the worried producer—who is sitting next to him in the company's private Jet Liner and sipping his fourth Martini. Frank lowers his seat to a reclining position and with slurred speech tells Jesse, "I didn't know salamanders hiss and have wings."

That was the end of their conversation until Frank awoke fourteen hours later with the words *Rang-Ta, Rang-Ta* on his lips. Once at the airport, Frank and Jesse give each other a strong hug, and Frank tells Jesse to take a week off until Frank talks to his bosses. "I'll be in touch then," he assures Jesse. And they part.

Jesse is worried and mulls over the situation, thinking, Frank doesn't know the meaning of the word *Rang-Ta*, yet, but he'll sure find out its meaning—and then what. If things get tough, I won't hesitate to call on the creature. I'm not about to jeopardize everything I've worked for. Frank might find himself hanging from a tree on the side of a mountain exactly as I did. This last thought gives Jesse some degree of comfort. He tries to sleep that night but his mind continues to race, so he reaches for a sleeping pill, and then another and another. He's drugged, but he sleeps.

❧

In the morning, Jesse calls a reliable, upper-class escort service and asks them to send a beautiful woman to his home. "The cost is unimportant," he says, "but hurry."

When the call girl appears, he is pleased. His need to be touched, held, caressed is insatiable. Only after three days of incessant lovemaking does he ask her name.

"My name is Gabrielle," she tells him, "but I need to rest. Aren't you a bit selfish?"

"What do you mean? I'm considerate of you."

"Yes, but let's leave this place for a few hours. I feel like I'm your prisoner. Let's go to dinner, a movie, the theatre—something different."

"Okay," says Jesse. "Go home, dress elegantly, and we'll go to dinner and the theatre. How's that?"

Two hours later, Gabrielle appears, dressed superbly and looking ravishing. Jesse falls at her feet and caresses her lower body as though he would devour her. Gabrielle loves the adoration and tells him that he is handsome.

They eat in a private room at an expensive restaurant. Forgetting that she is a whore, he looks at her adoringly. In the theatre, they laugh until their bodies hurt. Jesse is ecstatic—this is what he's been missing. This is what his body, mind, and soul need. He is falling in love. Should he take her home with him? Should he risk doing that? Will the creature show up? If only it wouldn't. Just one more night, one more night of delicious holding of her magnificent body, of cuddling with her, of loving her from head to feet, of being made love to in return. Oh, God, what must I do to have that?

I'll risk it, murmurs Jesse. "Come home with me, Gabrielle."

When they return to his home, he makes passionate love to her. Gabrielle responds, not like a whore, but like a woman, almost as desperate as Jesse is to be loved. They both become aware of each other's humanness, and this time when their eyes meet, the glow from their hearts is present. They become shy, embarrassed at what they're feeling.

Jesse gets out of bed, goes to the kitchen, and suggests he make hot chocolate for them. Gabrielle follows him, laughing hysterically. "I haven't had hot chocolate since I was in middle school."

"Nor have I," admits Jesse.

"Let's do it together," suggests Gabrielle.

"Okay," Jesse agrees, rummaging around in the cupboards for chocolate powder. When he finds some tucked away in the corner he is jubilant saying, "My housekeeper thinks of everything. Sit here on this chair while the water heats up. I'll look for some cake to go with it."

Gabrielle willingly does what he wants and smiles lovingly at him, at his handsomeness, his potent body, and right now at the innocence she sees in him. Jesse catches the love in her eyes. His heart feels the warmth of that love and he becomes aware that he would want to have that love all the time. They sit enjoying the hot chocolate and the cake he's found in the Frigidaire, each of them feeling as though they have just come to life.

A quick movement on the kitchen sink catches Jesse's eye. Is it pink? he asks himself. No, it can't be. You've got other converts to monitor, Natas. Why the hell always me? He protests silently. He dares to look again. Oh yes, it's pink all right—and growing bigger.

He turns to his companion. "Gabrielle," he yells hysterically, "I don't feel well. You've got to leave." He grabs her clothes and helps dress her. She's dumbfounded and speechless as Jesse opens the door to his home and pushes her out into the street. After grabbing a roll of bills, he again opens the door and throws the money after her. "Get a cab. Be sure to get a cab."

He returns to his bed, where the creature is already lying, salamander-size, at the foot of his bed. "Have you missed me?" it hisses sheepishly.

"Let's go to sleep," Jesse tells it in dejected resignation and for the first time in his life as a star, he feels that he would like to die.

Upon awakening, Jesse goes to the kitchen to make breakfast. The cups from Gabrielle's stay remain on the table. He sighs and almost cries, but Sal's entry into the kitchen stops his tears. Jesse notices that when Natas wishes to be friendly and unthreatening, it shows up as a salamander, which makes Jesse more relaxed in the creature's presence, and often the salamander's softness fosters a friendlier conversation.

"You're sad," remarks Natas, looking at Jesse with compassion. Jesse, uncertain whether Natas' feelings are feigned or real, is so vulnerable at this moment that any sympathy from anyone can touch him.

"Yes, Natas, I'm sad—sad without a woman who loves me. I'm beginning to wonder if my life with all of its riches is worth living.

Sal grinds its teeth ferociously—an indication to Jesse that it is repressing a lot of rage. "Well, now," replies Sal, masterfully controlled, "you know that in my kingdom, which is quickly becoming an empire (at which thought it gives a self-satisfied snort), marriage is not allowed. You know, I have a powerful competitor called *God* who sanctions such mundane alliances; and I do believe that as a result his kingdom is run less efficiently than mine. I want all my converts alert, available, and unhampered by marital affairs and problems."

"Not all marriages are besieged by so many problems that they would hamper the growth of your empire, Sal," explains Jesse, hoping to convince Natas' thinking. "You're right—from my youth, I too learned that God encourages marriage. He even created a woman out of one of Adam's ribs, so that Adam, the first man, wouldn't be alone. It's unnatural for a man to be without a companion. God encouraged his couples to procreate, to multiply themselves, to enhance his kingdom with offspring who are devoted to him. When a leader is loved by the populace, harmony exists. And what do you think harmony creates, Sal?"

Sal is listening attentively. The question throws him off guard. "Why, I don't know. I suppose you're right about the harmony idea; but in time people will want to take over the power for themselves. Everybody develops an ego sooner or later—and when that happens, the empire—will be destroyed because the populace has been given too much free will. I tell you that *free will leads to destruction, and I will not have an empire of free-willed people!*" Natas grows to its full dimension, its jaws grinding, its eyes and nostrils flaring forth fire. Clearly the creature is upset by the idea.

Jesse remains undaunted, continuing to speak even though Natas' gigantic head now is touching the ceiling, far away from Jesse's body and voice. Not caring whether he lives or dies, Jesse elucidates further, "You want solitary, prideful converts, then, without a loving nature; whose frustrated energy prey on others; who use cunning to force their will; who rape, murder, and steal to get their needs met; who, like cannibals, even physically devour others to satisfy their insatiability. You want your solitary converts to multiply haphazardly, conceiving loveless bastards who in turn avenge their own miserable natures and create misdeeds far worse than their predecessors." Jesse, the actor, is breathless and remains silent—deliberately staging a long, dramatic silence for effect. "You want them to be just like you."

Natas, still elongated and occupying the space between the floor and the ceiling, is flabbergasted. It quickly contracts its body and diminishes itself to Jesse's size with a loud, resounding crash, knocking over the chairs around the kitchen table. "Sorry, I must go now," Natas says, bewildered and apologetic. "I'm not angry at you, Jesse, for speaking your mind. It's good to do that sometimes. When I leave, however, take a cup from the cupboard and at your leisure look into it." With these words it disappears.

Jesse is astonished by his unusual candor with someone as grotesque and dangerous as Natas. "If I'd been able to express myself like this with you, Pop, when I was young, I wouldn't be hovering between life and death now." He knows that looking into the cup is Natas' response to his monologue. I'd better do what it says, thinks Jesse, unable to sustain his defiance. He gets a cup from the cupboard, turns one of the chairs right-side up and sits at the table looking into the cup.

A face appears, Jesse younger by twelve years. His appearance is shabby and unkempt. He is good-looking but his skin has acne and his arms have been slightly foreshortened since childhood—and he is totally despondent. Working as a waiter in a busy restaurant, Jesse is running around frantically serving the customers at his station. His immigrant boss who owns this greasy hellhole is a miserable personality just like his father. Jesse hates his job, hates his boss, but he depends on his work as a waiter to pay his bills. At night he goes to acting classes—exhausted, but mustering enough energy to do the work. The teachers tell him he's talented. Jesse knows he is talented; all he needs is a break. But how does an actor get a break when he's forced to work most of the day?

Jesse auditions for a small part in a soap opera on television. Just to be seen, he rationalizes. Maybe a producer will like my looks, remember me, and call me for another show.

The show gets filmed during his workday at the restaurant. He "calls in sick." The following day when he returns to his job, he is greeted by an irate boss. "You liar, scumbag, no-good liar, you wanna cheat me? I'll show you."

"What's up?" Jesse asks innocently.

"What's up?" the boss yells in front of all the customers. "Two of my customers saw you yesterday on that stupid soap show, playin' a cop. You were on for less than a second—and for that you don't show up for work, leaving me shorthanded at the last minute? They made a fool of me, you nincompoop liar, and then they rubbed your lie into my face: 'He made a fool of you, Pop,' they told me. 'He's supposed to be sick.' The owner gesticulates like the customers had and continues to rant: "For this you get nottin', nottin', from me—not even your tips. So scram, you bum. I never liked you anyway."

Jesse is dumbfounded. He yells ineffectually between portions of the boss's tirade, "Drop dead, immigrant, drop dead." He repeats these words like a mantra tumbling out of a dry, spastic throat—sounding like an apologetic whisper. Finally, the boss and two waiters push him out of the restaurant.

Jesse stumbles back to his apartment, morose, frightened, and humiliated. Once there he observes the shabbiness of his tiny room; and although he pays a pittance for the dwelling, he wonders how he will pay the next month's rent and be able to eat, too. He runs his hands through his dresser drawers looking for loose coins—none there. He turns his trousers pockets inside out, hoping to find some hidden money—none is found.

"God, if you exist," he yells, "where the hell are you? What do you want from me? Look at the parents you gave me. They weren't available to me—I have to do it all for myself. Is that fair? You're just like them; I can't count on you either. *I disown you.* From now on, you're out of my vocabulary. There is no God!"

Jesse stares into nothingness, feeling nothing—a blank, a void. The air is still, nothing is moving, even his breath does not breathe. 'Me, an actor?' he asks dourly. 'Who cares? Nothingness. Slit my wrists?—don't even have a sharp knife. Jump out of the window? Too gruesome! Take drugs? Don't have the money. I'll go back to the restaurant tomorrow and demand the pay I've earned and the tips that are mine.' He sleeps fretfully, filled with fear over confronting Pop—which pop is he struggling with? Both pops!

The next day, he faces the restaurant from across the street. No lights are on, no people are in it, other than a woman taping a sign to the door from the outside.

—DEATH OF OWNER—
RESTAURANT CLOSED INDEFINITELY

"How did he die?" Jesse asks, crossing the street to face her and disguising any emotion.

"Heart attack," the woman replied.

"Oh," Jesse says briskly as he turns and walks away.

Jesse is incredulous, then exuberant, then incredulous. My curse worked! My curse worked, even though I was a scared puppy. "What will you do now with all of your money, immigrant!" he declares to the air in front of him. "Drop dead all over again and in a lot of agony, lousy bastard!! Go to hell!" Jesse feels satisfied and returns to his apartment, gloating that justice has been done.

When he enters his apartment, the place has a different ambiance, less morbid—even hopeful. He spots a one-hundred-dollar bill lying on the table. Jesse grabs it, thinking that he had overlooked the money when he was scrounging around for coins. He pockets it quickly, anxious to feed his empty stomach.

On the way out, he's stopped by a whispering in his ears: first the right ear, then the left. The voice says, "There's more where this came from." Jesse shakes his head to relieve what he perceives to be a ringing in his ears. Sure, he thinks, the ringing must be from the stress of the events yesterday and today. He feeds himself royally—until his stomach gets bloated. When he returns, he sees more bills lying on the table. This time two hundred dollars. "Wow!" he exclaims, "This is no accident. Who's doing this? Who are you?"

A snorting, hissing, nasal voice answers quietly from the corner of his room. "You know me when you curse, condemn, and hate others. You know me, Jesse, especially when you damn my enemy—God. I like that! As long as he's no longer in your vocabulary, I'll take care of you. *All you have to do is listen to me! Only to me! Do you understand? Only to me!*"

"Okay, Okay," responds Jesse. "I'll listen to you. But, I'll test you first. I want a big role in a soap opera that will catch a producer's attention."

"You'll have to buy some clothes to impress a producer," says the nasal voice. With the utterance of this statement, bills come flying through the air. Jesse catches the money in both of his hands, all the while shrieking like a child who has finally been given something. When all the cash has been gathered together, Jesse says, "Gee, thanks." And then there is silence.

Jesse counts the bills, a huge sum of money—enough to get clothes, pay rent, and buy food. 'This is more than I ever got from either of you lousy parents. You too can drop dead from the worst disease imaginable. I'd feel good. I wouldn't even go to your funeral. I now have a daddy, a daddy without a body, but someone who's good to me. I wonder what this voice looks like. Doesn't matter, as long as it helps me.'

Jesse returns to his apartment fully dressed, stylish, and handsome—a handsomeness enhanced by a much-needed facial treatment that helped his acne plus a massage that elongated his muscles, giving them a normal appearance. "Look at me, voice, look at me! Now for a big part in a soap." The phone rings right away. At the other end is the assistant of the producer who had hired him to play a cop in the soap that had created so much havoc. "Because you resemble the star, Jesse, and he was just taken to the hospital, could you sub for him on this last-moment notice? You'll air later this afternoon?"

"Can I ever," replies Jesse. "I'll be there in thirty minutes."

⌘

Jesse had an arduous day at the television studio, but he is gleeful and satisfied with his success. He unlocks his apartment door wondering what will await him. That nasal voice greets him, but this time it emanates from a body enveloped in a thick, translucent haze, sitting on a chair by his kitchen table. Like a happy child, Jesse runs toward it—wishing to embrace it, to thank it, and to share the day's happenings. But as Jesse approaches and the specter becomes more clearly defined, Jesse gulps, and is thrown back into a nearby chair from shock and bewilderment.

Natas is attired in a pink suit with a white stiff collar around a bulging, thick crocodilian neck. Its head has the semblance of a crocodile but all of its features are modified so that Jesse is looking at an almost human face with crocodilian features. Its reptilian feet are shoved into pointy, leather shoes the same color as his outfit, and of course its wings and tail are pink.

Jesse, pale from disbelief and mouth ajar, fixates on this creature, his eyes scanning it from head to foot. "Are you the one who's been giving me the money?" he asks, stuttering uncontrollably.

"Yes, Jesse. Don't be surprised by what you see. I'm not the average-looking, um, person…or man…or creature you might expect. And of course this is not my usual appearance either. When we become better acquainted I'll show you the true me. Natas is my name, Jesse, and you can call me by that name starting right now." Natas extends toward Jesse its two upper appendages, which immediately fuse into two long arms and hands on either side of its body. The apparition's fingers are extremely long, the fingernails pointy and polished with bright pink enamel.

"All right, Natas," says Jesse, still stuttering as he timidly places his right hand into Natas' outstretched hands, which feel unexpectedly soft and therefore less of an ordeal to touch. The actor within Jesse pretends that he is confronting a creature from a scene in *Alice in Wonderland*. This enables him to adjust more easily than most people could to this grotesque interplay and to ask Natas more genuinely, "How did you discover me? How did you know I was down and out?"

"Oh, my dear Jesse," sniffs Natas, "that's a secret that only I and God know about. The more important question is, now that I've discovered a potential convert, will you let me have your soul to do with as I will? You've had a preview of what's in store for you, and there's more to come. But, before you answer, tell me, Jesse, how did things go today?"

Natas settles uncomfortably into the chair, having difficulty placing its tail and wings. He realizes, however, that this being their first interview, it is so important to sacrifice its comfort and to win Jesse's soul. It sits rigidly in the chair feigning relaxation and ease.

More himself, Jesse now turns into a young boy describing the events of the day to Natas, who has become 'the good poppa.' "The star is very sick," he explains, pretending sympathy. "They told me I'm a better actor with a better personality, and handsomer." Jesse lowers his head shyly giving his report to his attentive listener. "Not only that, but the producer wants me to be available until further notice. *And*—my salary will be two thousand five hundred dollars a week."

Natas snorts, sniffs and grinds its teeth, all of these sounds, an indication of its interest and approval. "But what will you do if the star recovers?"

"I don't know," answers Jesse thoughtfully. "I don't wish to put a curse on him as I did with the restaurant owner. It worked and I'm not sorry." At this moment, Jesse eyes the creature innocently.

Natas catches Jesse's subtle inference and holds its breath. "Do you want me to take care of the matter?"

Jesse struggles briefly with his conscience. "Would you, Natas?"

Natas, folding its right wing in front of its body, reaches into an opening in the wing that holds a miniscule syringe. "You know, Jesse, nothing is for nothing. If you want my loyalty, you will have to give me your soul unconditionally. I'll draw a drop of blood from my heart and place it into your heart. This will give me the assurance that God no longer is in your heart and that *I, only I, reign there.* This will seal our pact."

"And then what?"

"And then, my dear boy, I will fulfill your wishes as you ask them."

"You will? No questions asked?"

"Of course!" affirms Natas as it draws a drop of blood from its heart and approaches Jesse for the soul bond. Jesse opens his shirt—*and the deed is done.* Natas' blood is running through Jesse's body; they are fused. Natas murmurs to itself that this bonding was easier than expected, turns around, and then disappears without another word.

Jesse looks around his apartment, but Natas is gone. Well, that was simple, he thinks; and if this is your modus operandi, being beholden to you will be simple too. Then he remembers that his rehearsal call is early the next morning, that it will be a long day…and that Natas "will take care of the matter." He sleeps soundly.

His presence at the television studio is approved by all the people on the set. They find Jesse easy to work with, quick with directions, and a good actor. At the end of the day's "shoot," the producer—looking somber—calls him into his office. Jesse feels devastated. He's certain that the job has ended and the star is returning and that Natas has betrayed him. Instead, the producer tells him that the star had unexpected health complications during the night and suddenly died that morning. The producer had decided not to convey this sad news to Jesse or the rest of the cast until after the shoot ended.

Jesse looks appropriately sad, but at the same time hears from the producer that the role is his if he wants it. Jesse and the producer sign a contract, shake hands, and when in the studio again, the cast cheers the new star.

His increased salary is astronomical, so Jesse relocates to a beautiful apartment. His sexual drive is consummated with many women, all of whom he rejects in time as his ardor turns into hatred. He is alone, living for his work as an actor. He has no friends; not even Natas has appeared in two years. Jesse becomes bored by his role and wants a career in film.

Before long, his fame and exposure in the soap opera world bring Jesse an offer to act in a film; but it requires a release from his present contract. The producer refuses to free him. Jesse is bound to their agreement for another three years, which makes him desperate. He calls for Natas' help—but it does not respond. Insane with fury, Jesse goes to a church to ask God for help—forgetting that he had abandoned God a few years earlier. On his knees, he hears, "You've given your heart to Satan, Jesse. You cannot have it both ways."

When Jesse leaves the church, he is more upset than ever. His fame has brought out his petulance, greed, and narcissism, just the way it always was, he wails inwardly. 'Forget I asked *you* for anything, God.' Out loud he hurls his deadly curse: "Drop dead, God, drop dead! I should have known better than to come to you."

⤚

At home, Jesse broods with a black despair and fury that instantaneously withers the foliage and flowers of his beautiful plants on the sunlit windowsills. Looking at their dying leaves and blooms, he wonders about his toxic energy, and screams, "Natas, show up or I'll get a blood transfusion, a total one so that your drop of blood is wiped out of my system forever. What good is a pact with you when you're unavailable?"

Jesse's curses echo in the otherwise silent apartment, where he is sitting on a luxurious, custom-made, green velvet couch smothered by pastel-colored pillows. Out of nowhere Jesse hears the nasal, hissing voice of Natas, which is having difficulty materializing itself.

"Where the hell have you been? I haven't seen you in two years. What kind of pacts do you make?" Jesse hollers into the air, waiting for a familiar form to appear. A salamander scoots across his thighs. "Eek,"

24

Jesse screeches, wanting to stomp out the creature if he could catch it. "No, no, don't kill me—it's me, Natas."

"Where are you?"

"At your feet. I'll get bigger so that you can see me." With that, Natas grows bigger and bigger until it occupies the entire height of the room.

Jesse screams out in fright. "You were ghastly enough to look at when I first saw you. What are you doing now?"

"I've forgotten how I appeared to you two years ago, Jesse. Forgive me if I'm frightening you. Now let me diminish my size to yours and we'll talk.

"Hello, Jesse," says the huge head and mouth in great agitation. "I've been exceedingly busy and you were doing well until now, so I let you be. What's your will?"

For an unknown reason, Jesse can't allow himself to tell Natas his concerns. He senses that although Natas is behaving friendly enough, the creature has an ominous, eerie tone to its voice. Paralyzed, Jesse cannot speak.

Natas' response to Jesse's viciousness is delayed as it tries to remember in what guise it had appeared to him back then. Once Natas remembers, it snaps fiercely at the two-year convert: "I'm not your servant whom you can use and misuse as you please. You called on God—didn't you—*knowing* he's my worst enemy. Our blood tie doesn't matter to you. I can't tolerate such betrayal! Besides I will not allow you to yell at me!"

Jesse opens his mouth to make excuses—the stress about the contract, his desire to do a film, the unwillingness of the producer... His attempts to explain himself make Natas more furious until Jesse feels himself picked up roughly by an unknown force at the back of his neck. His whole body is whisked through the air, air sometimes frigid as ice, sometimes ablaze from the torrid sun, sometimes drenched as though hit by a deluge of rain. Then he comes to a stop, suspended on the branch of a tree that is jutting out of the side of a huge mountain. What mountain is this, what country is this? wonders Jesse. But what does it matter? he realizes. When he looks down to the earth a few thousand feet below the perch he's hanging from, he gasps in horror—nothing else matters.

"Natas, I promise I'll never, ever betray you again," Jesse implores. "I didn't recognize how much you've done for me and how fortunate I am to have you, Natas," Jesse pleads hoarsely until the sun goes down. All through the night he hangs on the branch, and in the morning he is too exhausted, too rigidified from terror to plead further with his tormentor. He faints.

When Jesse awakens, he is lying on his green couch in his apartment—pale and weak. Natas looks into his face, urging him to drink the glass of water it holds before him. Jesse peers suspiciously at Natas, turns away, and sobs convulsively. "I didn't mean to hurt you," he sobs. "I didn't mean to hurt you." Natas is appeased.

"You've learned who's the master of your life, haven't you, Jesse?"

Jesse nods his head. They sit quietly together while Jesse explains his dilemma. The creature's gargantuan crocodilian head is ablaze with interest, accompanied by sniffing, snorting, and grinding of its teeth. By the time Jesse has uttered his last sentence, the creature no longer is by his side, it has disappeared.

Jesse rises from the couch and squeals unthinkingly, "My God, thank you! I mean, *Natas,* thank you. Thank you from my heart. I mean our heart. Oh, rats, what do I mean? I mean I'm happy to be alive and I'll never jeopardize our relationship again!" Jesse's bravado is momentarily tamed and replaced by the demeanor of a relieved little boy.

For the next two weeks, Jesse continues working at the studio just like before. When nothing changes in that period of time, Jesse begins doubting Natas' loyalty and becomes fretful and miserable yet again. He doesn't throw a tantrum, however; the last experience taught him a memorable lesson. At the end of the second week, impatient with everything—the rehearsals, the melodrama of his scripts, the people on the set, his producer, the long hours—he decides to remind Natas of its promises in a gentle, thoughtful, sensitive way. But it is now Jesse who is grinding his teeth from frustration and an overwhelming desire to destroy Natas. While in his dressing room, and not a moment too soon, Jesse is saved from another debacle with the fiend. An attorney at the studio comes up to Jesse and hands him an official envelope. The paper inside has a notice from the producer informing him:

THE STUDIO IS CLOSED—CHAPTER 11.
ALL CONTRACTS ARE TERMINATED
UNTIL FURTHER NOTICE

Jesse rushes to the telephone and in minimal time, his career as a film actor begins.

❦

Back near the pond, Gabrielle sits in awe, spellbound by what she has seen in Natas' eyes. The creature waits for her to come out of her stupor. Finally she asks, "Who is Jesse? Why are you showing me his life?"

"You don't know him, Gabrielle?" asks Natas, "You really don't know him?"

"No." She hesitates long enough to clarify her thoughts. "I'm a woman; he's some man I don't know. Why should I be interested in his life? Except that I do find him attractive, talented, and successful. He and I share a lot of similarities: his background, my background. I too changed my name from Sara to Gabrielle—more Anglo-Saxon. I used to call my father "Poppa." He does too. My father is a distant, cold man, an immigrant from Europe—just like Jesse's. My Poppa always thought I was beautiful and he has a 'thing' for me, which is probably an incestuous 'thing.' Although I don't remember clearly, it feels like incest. That's probably why my mother couldn't stand me and made my life miserable." Gabrielle sheds a few tears as she recalls her past.

"Don't cry, Gabrielle," Natas tells her while it unexpectedly assumes the form of a salamander lying at her feet. Surprised, Gabrielle strokes the top of its head. The attention gives Natas so much enjoyment that the creature almost purrs. It feels vulnerable around her, so it quickly changes its form into the dapper Natas in a pink suit and stiff white collar that first appeared to Jesse.

Is this creature in competition with Jesse? Gabrielle asks herself, smiling. She finds all of Natas' guises amusing and tells him that she feels like a child in Disneyland. Delighted, Natas continues his machinations to please her. She laughs uproariously. "You know I'm enjoying you as I would enjoy a friend."

"I like that, Gabrielle. Why can't we become friends? You know I didn't always look like this. When God first created me, the heavenly hosts referred to me as a prince. I was strong, handsome—more handsome than Jesse—and powerful. I was God's favorite angel, until… until…that's another story." Natas saddens as it recalls the days of long ago. "But things change and I guess I reflect on the outside what's happening on the inside." It grinds its teeth and snorts as though in pain, yet quickly dismisses any feelings of remorse. "That's the past, and the present and future are what's important," it continues in a businesslike manner. "Do you want to be my friend?"

"I'll see," Gabrielle answers. "I don't want to end up hanging from a tree off the side of a mountain as Jesse did."

"That kind of thing only happens when humanity takes me for granted," replies Natas. "It happens when humanity wants the fruits of the vine without the willingness to till the soil."

"Well, I've tilled the soil all of my life. Working hard is nothing new for me. You know, I left college before I finished and got a job to help my parents. And I've been working ever since. Presently, I work in a department store: I'm bored, miserable, and never have enough money. If only I had finished my education, I would be a more qualified person now." There is a long pause.

"What's wrong?" asks Natas, concerned.

"I have to make a confession. When I'm short of money, I get it from a man. I guess I'm a whore of sorts. But, I can't even make that work—I choose losers."

With a sigh of relief, Natas asks, "You were lying when you told me you didn't know Jesse? Why?"

"I'm ashamed, Natas, at the meaningless of my life. After the last loser—to whom I gave and gave with no rewards—I decided to go for big-time prostitution. I called the escort service; they interviewed me, liked me, and called me for my first job. And that first job was Jesse. He was insatiable. We spent a number of days together, and then he threw me out, shoving a bundle of bills out of the door after me. I was so humiliated that I took my name off their list. This is the truth, Natas. But I sure envy Jesse's male aggression. He's ambitious, knows how to get what he wants, and probably has more money than he needs."

"You admire Jesse, you say?" snorts Natas. "Would you like to meet him again?"

"Sure, why not? I don't have the clothes or the finesse, though. But, why should he want to meet me again, after he threw me out of his home?"

"Don't worry about that. The clothes and finesse are not a problem either. Go home, look into your closet and wear what you see. Tell the escort service you're available. Jesse always calls them. You've been accepted by them because you're gorgeous. You'll be rediscovered by Jesse."

"Why are you hooking me up with him? I thought you didn't believe in couples?"

"I don't," says Natas, "but this will be different—special you might say." It chuckles strangely.

Gabrielle shudders.

"You refuse?"

"Well, um…I'm in a rut…maybe this will get me out of the rut."

Natas looks at her quietly. This will be your first adventure under my supervision. If you like it and will want more, you will have to ally yourself with my heart as Jesse did. And your soul will be mine. That's my offer."

"I'd like to try this first adventure. I'm scared of being thrown out again, but I'm willing to try. And then I'll see if I want to give you my soul."

Natas bids her goodbye and disappears.

Gabrielle returns to her apartment and reinstates herself with the escort service. When she walks over to look in her closet, she howls with pleasure at the striking clothing she discovers. She tries on one stunning outfit after another, each one complete with shoes, hat, handbag, gloves, perfume, as well as lingerie. Looking at herself in the mirror, she proclaims silently, if I'm going to be a whore, I might as well be a high-class one and make a lot of money so I can leave that damned department store. As for you, Poppa and Momma, the free ride is over. I've done it too long; it's time to think of myself.

But, what am I getting into? Give my soul to Natas and be harnessed to him for the rest of my life? My soul is mine, even though I've been too weak to direct myself. Maybe I'll find out what motivates Jesse and learn from him how to be more dynamic in my life. His background is no different from mine. If he can do it, so can I. Gabrielle gains clarity as she stands before the mirror arguing with herself and her conscience. And now I'll wait for the next step in this adventure.

The next step happens the very next day. Gabrielle looks devastatingly beautiful when she rings Jesse's doorbell. He opens the door, a phone in hand, deeply immersed in a business conversation. He barely looks at her, guiding her with his free hand into the living room, and he tells her to make herself comfortable while he continues his conversation elsewhere.

Gabrielle is familiar with his home and heads for the bar, making them each a drink. She takes her glass, sets it on a small table beside a luxurious sofa, and slowly removes her outer garment—a designer creation made of silks and satins. It covers an elegant dress that shows off the slimness of her body, and the colors enhance Gabrielle's dark complexion and long dark hair, now tied loosely into a knot touching her shoulders.

Waiting for Jesse to finish his phone call, Gabrielle reflects on his blue eyes, the same shade of blue as hers. She instantly remembers that the only way either of her parents could fathom why their daughter had blue eyes was that she was not their child—rather she was a mistake, a switch made by one of the attendants in the hospital. Gabrielle recalls her parents' words and their ugly insinuations. She tries to soothe herself with not your child, huh? You're right. I'm too special to come from your seed. You should see me now, both of you. You treated me like a Cinderella. Well, Cinderella is meeting her Prince Charming—my Cinderella days are over. My efforts are wasted on you; fend for yourselves and plead poverty and old age to someone else who'll be willing to take care of you.

Slowly sipping her drink, she tries to remember how many years ago she sat in this same living room. 'Three years or four?' she questions, counting on her fingers. She's unaware that Jesse is standing at the room's entrance watching her. When she turns around to face him, he screams with delight, "Is it you, Gabrielle?"

"It's me—the woman you threw out a few years ago."

"I remember and I'm sorry," he responds quietly. "I was hit by a virus."

"No virus, Jesse," she tells him quietly, gliding toward him and into his arms.

They kiss ravenously, and without further discussion he carries her into his bedroom. After their passion has been satiated, Jesse tells her how vividly he remembers their last time together. "No one's felt like you since. I want you again, Gabrielle," he croaks hoarsely.

"Take me, Jesse, I'm all yours."

"Oh, God, you're magnificent and we fit so well. It's scary, isn't it?"

"Not really, Jesse," Gabrielle answers knowingly. "It's how it should be."

"I can't get enough of you—everything about you—your smell, how your skin feels, your beauty. I'm lucky."

"You talk too much," Gabrielle tells him. "Let me love you now." And she does. His blue eyes shine radiantly as he submits to her gentle, loving caresses. Neither of them can get enough of the other as their lovemaking continues into the morning.

Gabrielle awakens first and scampers to the kitchen. Jesse follows, and she orders him to sit at the table. "We never did finish that hot chocolate and cake," Gabrielle tells him smilingly. "Shall we do it now?" Jesse laughs hysterically that she remembers; and, had it not been for their extreme hunger, they would have returned to bed to quench again their ardent desire for each other.

At first he sits quietly, awestruck by the feelings in his heart. He watches every movement Gabrielle makes: reaching for a plate in the uppermost part of the cupboard, which exposes her bare, shapely legs and thighs; the outline of her delicate breasts against her robe; how her long hair flows with every movement she makes. He could have watched her indefinitely. 'How hungry I am for love,' Jesse remarks to himself. And then abruptly and without warning Jesse's fear strikes. He becomes fidgety and scans the kitchen for any signs of a pink, moving creature. Gabrielle senses his discomfort and tells him, "Relax, honey, nothing will take away our time together, and you won't have to throw me out, either."

Jesse gives a chuckle of relief, but at the same time throws a questioning look in her direction, wondering, What does she know? Why shouldn't I be apprehensive? Why is she so sure nothing will happen?

Gabrielle sits in his lap and strokes his blond hair, kissing his blue eyes with a gusto that makes him giggle. Being with her is so satisfying that Jesse forgets about Natas. In fact, he puts on music, and they dance and hold each other until Jesse tells Gabrielle he is due at the film studio. "Don't leave. Be here when I come back."

"Shall I make dinner?"

"Good idea. Here's some money." Jesse leaves his home happier than he's ever been.

Gabrielle is delighted, and she calls for Natas to reveal its whereabouts and intentions so that she can lessen Jesse's fears. The creature comes to Gabrielle as a salamander.

"You're happy, Gabrielle?" it asks. "I want that for you. I won't appear unless you call for me." It leaves.

❦

Jesse returns from the studio that evening, and once again he feasts his eyes on Gabrielle while she prepares a special meal for the two of them. His ooh's and aah's with every taste of the food gives her great pleasure. They chat and laugh. Jesse tells her of the incident that occurred during the shoot that day: He had mistakenly called his leading lady "Gabrielle," and the cast teased him mercilessly, whispering "Jesse's in love with Gabrielle. Jesse's in love with Gabrielle. He's a transformed man." She notices that he seldom looks around for the apparition; but when he does, she sees terror in his face.

"Should we go to a movie?" asks Jesse as though he is on his first date. Tomorrow's my day off. We have tonight and tomorrow before the next shoot takes place." He finishes with an apology: "Then I'll have to get a lot of rest, otherwise the camera will pick up my wrinkles, which would hurt my career."

"Okay, Jesse. Let's play until tomorrow evening, and then I'll leave so that you can have your rest."

"You're perfect, Gabrielle," Jesse tells her and picks her up and takes her to his bedroom. At the threshold, Jesse suddenly becomes disquieted, his fear running high. He looks around the room like a madman, peering into every corner for anything that might resemble Natas' pink form. Jesse reaches for Gabrielle's body, but his potency has vanished. Gabrielle fondles his genitals to arouse him sexually, but his organ remains flaccid. He growls like a beast from frustration and humiliation and silently blames his partner.

"It's okay, Jesse, it's okay."

Embarrassed and angry, he lies with his back toward Gabrielle. Finally he falls asleep, believing that his impotency is her fault. This has never happened, ever, he reassures himself. 'What can I expect from a hooker? A whore! Of course, that's it! My heart is involved with a prostitute, who would be only play-acting. After all, it's what she gets paid for. In the morning, I'll tell her to leave—this time for good. I'm too good to be with a whore. Yeah, that's it. Why did I let my heart fall for her? Why? She's familiar, that's why. And we're good together, but, that's in bed. We've got to have more in common. What does she do for a living besides being a good hooker? She makes good meals. She's beautiful to look at, and I love her body. But, that's not enough. See what she's doing to my potency. She's got to go!'

The next morning Jesse awakens to the aroma of brewing coffee, freshly made muffins, eggs and sausages. When he pokes his head into the kitchen, he sees the busy chef dressed in his old sweatshirt, looking ravishing. He's naked and calls her to him. When she approaches and he embraces her, she feels a contracted, rigid body—a body stiff with apprehension. He senses that once again his genital will not obey his passionate feelings for Gabrielle. Like a frantic animal, he dashes to the table and devours the food she has presented on his plate. She sits opposite him and eats slowly, tasting everything she has prepared and silently wondering about his uncouth behavior. He is resolute about dismissing her, but her loving smile deters the harsh pronouncement.

"Jesse, Jesse, it's okay, believe me."

His blue eyes melt. "It's okay for you, but not for me."

"I know what you're capable of. Sometimes the body needs a rest. You're not a machine."

"Yeah, that's it. My body needs a rest. Why don't you leave now, Gabrielle. I'll call you soon. How about that?"

"If that's what you want," Gabrielle says passively, disappointed that once again she's being sent away. I'll leave after I clean up."

"No, no, don't do that. My cleaning woman will take care of everything. Just leave and I'll get some rest."

Gabrielle goes to his side, but he pushes her away.

"Okay, Jesse, call me." Distraught, she dresses and leaves his house.

Damn it, Jesse declares to himself, it's either Natas that scares the hell out of me or a woman for whom I have some feelings. I'm not the man I was.

After a few hours of ruminating about his plight and rationalizing that his sexual disturbance is Gabrielle's fault, he calls the escort service to send a different woman. They ask if the last one was unsatisfactory. "No," he tells them. "I need variety."

Jesse has sex with the new prostitute. His abilities are as usual—that is, sex is an emotionless act with a number of ejaculations while he manipulates an abstract body underneath him, but whose name he doesn't know. It's that woman, Gabrielle, he convinces himself. Nothing is wrong with me. That'll be the last time I'll call on her.

He gives the new whore money for a taxi, shuts the door behind her, and makes sure he gets his rest so that his face will not acquire more wrinkles.

Upon returning to the film studio the next day, Jesse struts around making sexual jokes. The cast and crew are incredulous, wondering why he's talking like a sexual pervert.

Gabrielle leaves Jesse's home in tears. She wants to take a cab to her apartment, but she is penniless. She had contributed her own money to their meal, and since no reimbursement or taxi money was offered, she must walk. She vehemently rejects the idea of returning and demanding the money she's owed.

Clothed in her fancy outfit and high heels, Gabrielle makes her way home—sometimes stumbling on the uneven stones of the sidewalks, sometimes sitting on stoops, lamenting miserably at her fate. At this moment she hates Jesse, life, and mostly herself. It's true what they tell me, she assumes, the old familiar words resounding in her head: You'll never amount to much, so don't bother with an education. Be practical. A job in a department store is better—you get benefits. College won't do anything for you. The neighbor's daughter downstairs on the fourth floor finished college, and she's no better off than you. Stay where you are, and be happy you've got a job. Besides, we need your help. Do you want us to be thrown into the streets? You know how hard Poppa works—and for what, for nothing.

Gabrielle hides her face in her hands and sobs deeply as the thoughts run rampantly around in her brain. But she can't sob for long, because in this dangerous neighborhood she must be aware of perverted people—whether someone behind a curtained window or a violent person walking in the streets with nowhere to go and looking for trouble.

At least I've got an apartment—dingy, tiny, and infested as it is with roaches and mice. It's a place to go to, anyway, she considers. She continues walking. Oh, Jesse, you pathetic monster, you want love, but you can't handle it when it's available. I thought I could learn from you how to be more successful—but all I see is a deceitful person who can't face the truth about himself. And I thought I loved you. Yeah, I loved a frightened boy.

By now Gabrielle is climbing the five flights of stairs to her tenement apartment. This is all I can afford, she despairs, what with giving a good amount of my salary to them—those ungrateful wretches that call themselves parents.

She picks up her mail in a dimly lit vestibule where most of the mailboxes hang off their hinges after being burglarized. Fortunately, her mailbox remains intact. My much-needed check from the escort service should be in this envelope, she tells herself. Oh, and here's another envelope from the department store; I hope they accepted my sick leave while I was with Jesse.

When she opens the door to her apartment and turns on the light, she hears mice skittering, looking for a safer hideout. The roaches, too, run back to their crevices to wait for the lights to be turned off so that they can resume their plundering.

Gabrielle, totally forlorn, sits down on a rickety chair and opens her department store envelope:

> All of our salespeople must maintain a sales rating in line with the standards of the department. We regret to say that due to your below-average rating, we must terminate your employment in this store. Your recent absence contributed to the above firm decision made by the store manager. You will not be given other employment in this store.

When she sees the amount of the enclosed check, she screams aloud, "You bastards—greedy, lousy bastards. All the years I spent there. I hate you." Gabrielle is stunned and sits fixed in one position until she snaps out of her stupor and opens the second envelope.

> We cannot pay you for your services to Jesse Jason. Our records indicate that merely a few hours after you left his premises, he called for a different escort. Clearly, he was dissatisfied with your service and, therefore, we do not feel obligated to pay you. Bad service to our clients is not only humiliating to our agency but gives it a bad name. Do not call us again.

Gabrielle wails to the ceiling, "You called for another escort, Jesse, after all that transpired between us? You must be crazy! God, if you exist, tell me what's going on. Tell me, before I lose my sanity. This is unfair, it's evil. I've given abundantly to Jesse. I've given plenty to the department store. I've given incessantly to my parents. Why is this happening to me? Why? Why?" Gabrielle falls to her knees, pleading, sobbing, unable to fathom Jesse's cruelty, unable to understand the cruelty of others.

She rips off her whoring clothes and takes a shower—scrubbing her body until her skin is raw, all the while mumbling, "I want to wash your cruelty to me off my body, your use of me, you pathetic, scared little boy. Star? Star of what? Star of wickedness!"

Gabrielle's pain cries out for justice, "Nobody, *nobody* is going to use me again, do you hear out there?—world full of beasts, full of hateful people—*nobody*, never again!"

She goes to bed, her rage ignited and at a high intensity. She sleeps as though she is wrestling with demons, punching them with her arms and kicking them mercilessly.

In the morning Gabrielle notices that her bedding is damp and bloodstained from her enraged ardor—her bedding, a general mess. What in the world happened here? she wonders. She notices bruises on her fingers and impulsively scratches her pillow once again, as though it was Jesse's body. "I sure hate you, little boy," she yells. "Ohhhh, how I hate, hate, hate!"

Gabrielle sees the meager check from the department store lying on her table and knows she can't survive on this pittance. At a loss, she pats ointment on her bruises and stares into a corner of the small room. Turning her gaze directly toward a place in the air, she screams aloud, "You didn't answer me last night when I begged for your help. Where are you? Is your enigmatic silence supposed to infuse me with holy wonder? Should I grovel on my knees to you? Should I exude the faith of Job, of Daniel, of Jesus—any of the saints—before you'll answer? Well, I'm none of them: I'm me, Gabrielle, a desperate human being, a whore, a weak slob whose life is pitiful." She silently waits. But the silence remains silent.

"Okay, God, I give up. I'll call on Natas. What good is my soul to me when I'm not important to you or to anyone else, when I beg and beg yet you don't hear me? What good is it to live life with honesty and integrity, and have abuse be my reward? I loved you, Jesse. I gave my heart and body to you, but you stomped on it. Well, I can play your game, too—and I will, because good, passive Gabrielle doesn't exist anymore. And you, parents, you'll have to live in the streets. Too bad! You also gave me nothing, so rot in your pretended poverty." Emotionally spent, Gabrielle sits mute on the only chair in her apartment.

She hears, "Gabrielle, Gabrielle, you have free will. Whatever lessons you need to learn are yours to be learned. I have not forsaken you. Do not forsake *me*."

"Words, words," she responds, "You're not going to come through. At least Natas appears when I call it. You play a 'maybe' game. Pray, plead, beg—until *you* are ready. Well, I've waited all of my life. I'm asking *now*."

"I am here in this room, child. Just be quiet and listen."

Gabrielle tries to listen. She is overwrought, however, and what she perceives is the snorting, sniffing, grunting of Natas in a distant corner—invisible, but willing to materialize when she abandons God.

Her ears ring, yet the heavenly signal is meaningless to her. A thunderous voice rumbles in her brain, but she is deaf to it. Out of nowhere, the perfume of roses fills the air, but she is unaware. Instead, Gabrielle continues to focus on her pain, resentment, and fury.

She does hear the gnashing of teeth, though, and finally says the dreaded and final words, "Come in, Natas. I want to make a pact with you." At which Natas swiftly materializes.

"I'm so glad you're calling, Gabrielle." It was happy to be by her side.

"Life is not working out for me, Natas," Gabrielle tells the creature, speaking to it like a friend. "I don't have to explain what happened with Jesse, do I? You knew when you had us meet."

"Well, um," snorts Natas. "I do know my clients and you had to experience the matter; otherwise, it would have been an insignificant adventure. You're miserable and angry, Gabrielle, at being used. That's good. Now, what is your wish?"

"I want success. I want to be strong and decisive and to have a luxurious life."

"That's easy," Natas assures her. "Shall we bond?"

"Oh, Natas, I'm not sure about the bond between us. Will it be forever?" Gabrielle's lips quiver.

"In your case, Gabrielle, for as long as you want."

"Really! I thought it is for eternity."

Shrugging aside her response, Natas tells her to get ready for their ritual. The tiny syringe is filled with a drop of Natas' blood and quickly injected into Gabrielle's heart. *They are fused.* Resonating from all of her pain, she reasons that whatever the future holds for her, her life will be less horrendous than it has been. "Okay, okay, Natas, it's done. Now what?"

"In the morning, dress chicly and go to this elegant jewelry store in the fashionable part of the city. Ask for a position with them. They will not refuse you, I promise." And with that said, Natas disappears.

⇄

After her interview, Gabrielle already has been invited to work behind a counter filled with precious gems: diamonds, rubies, sapphires, and more—all set into necklaces, rings, bracelets, and other artful adornments. The counter sparkles, and so does Gabrielle's beauty. All who pass by are awed.

An elderly gentleman, tall and good-looking with gray hair, circles the counter, looking at a ring in the case and then at Gabrielle. Finally he asks her with great sincerity to help him choose a ring for a friend. She selects the most extraordinary ring in the store, bejeweled with a huge diamond centered in a platinum setting, surrounded by smaller exquisite diamonds. She removes it from the case.

"Would you mind putting it on your finger?" he requests. When she has done so, he stands apart from her, in deep appreciation of the ring, her fingers, her hands, and the arm that flows into a shapely body and a sublime face. Gabrielle becomes embarrassed at the man's unabashed admiration. He then circles the counter again, glancing casually at other counters and walking to them to observe other pieces of jewelry. Gabrielle stands quietly, not knowing what to do.

He returns to her counter and beams at her. After removing a checkbook from the inside pocket of his custom-made jacket, the man writes a check for the astronomical cost of the ring. All this is done without hesitation.

"To whom shall I send it?" Gabrielle asks nervously.

"I'd like it to be sent to you," he tells her. And before she can absorb the meaning of his words, he disappears.

Gabrielle is confounded, looking at the ring on her finger, searching for the man who just left, wishing to ask, "What do you mean?" She asks her manager what she should do: he recognizes the name on the check and mentions that the gentleman is one of the richest men in the world.

"Do nothing, Gabrielle. Wear the ring—that's all. Be sure to wear it every day, because he'll return, I guarantee it."

Gabrielle is embarrassed and needs to ask, "Since it's not safe where I live, may I leave it in one of the store's safety deposit boxes overnight and wear it when I return the next day?"

"Good idea, Gabrielle. But, be sure to wear it; otherwise he'll be angered, and he is too valuable a customer to lose."

Gabrielle does as she is told even though she is totally flabbergasted. Her appreciation of the gem on her finger grows, and she tries to change her wardrobe daily to accentuate this work of art. Before long, *she* has become the showpiece of the store. People enter the premises purely to stare at her beauty and the ring on her finger.

The following week the stately man appears again, circles her counter, looks at her from head to foot, and tells her she has good taste. Finding so much adulation difficult to handle, Gabrielle blushes like a vestal virgin. Then he looks at necklaces, muttering to himself, "A necklace that complements the ring," as Gabrielle tries to help him. He suddenly looks into her eyes and asks, "Which necklace would you choose?"

"Um, this one," she replies while pointing to the most elaborate, the most expensive, and of course the most exquisite.

"Put it on," he commands. Again and again he circles the counter, never taking his eyes off the vision behind it. He glibly writes another check, the figure more astronomical than before. "You're made in heaven," he tells her, handing her the check, and then he leaves.

The manager has been watching the entire transaction, his breath stuck in his throat, hoping that Gabrielle will do the right thing— which she does. He waits patiently for the customer to leave and takes the check from a flushed Gabrielle. "Do what he says, Gabrielle. Always wear what he has given you. And at night leave them in our safety deposit box."

Gabrielle's heart suddenly flutters with misgivings at his last statement; she's no longer innocent of the machinations of mankind. "I believe you know that this jewelry belongs to me, given to me by Mr. Jiran. I want a personal safety deposit box, the combination of which will be known only to me. The box will store my jewelry and I will have access to it whenever I please. Tomorrow when I come to the store I will open the box myself, and by then I will have papers in my possession drawn up by an attorney ascertaining that these gifts are mine. Is all of this clear?"

The manager reddens and perspires heavily, for Gabrielle is looking into his scheming mind. "Of course, of course, as you wish." He returns to his station dumbfounded. But he silently thinks otherwise, Okay, sister, you play innocence and simplicity, but I'll get you for speaking to me like an equal. Then he invokes a hideous curse on her—which registers on Gabrielle's body like a stab in the back. She shrugs it off, returns to her work and quietly affirms, 'Nobody, nobody's going to use me again.'

Other customers come to her counter, buy small items, engage her in conversation, and are charmed by her.

Although she feels like a circus exhibit, she does delight in the public's attention. She thinks to herself, you should see me now, Momma and Poppa. The world thinks I'm beautiful. You told me I was ugly with an ugly nose. I'm trying to believe what the world says, but why is it so hard?

The manager, too, watches her at all times, making notes of any infraction of the rules. He's become her enemy, but she doesn't care because she knows she can rely on Natas to handle him. You're my personal champion, Natas. Doesn't everyone need that kind of support in a world like this? she says to herself convincingly.

Supported by her thoughts, she turns to her next customer and smiles beatifically. They cannot resist buying from her. She gloats at the amount of sales she has made that day and figuratively thumbs her nose at the bad evaluation given her from her previous job.

Gabrielle thinks of Mr. Jiran, who hasn't appeared in two weeks. Perhaps she'll surprise him by picking out earrings and a bracelet to match what he has already given her. She selects the most gorgeous items and tucks them in a special part of the bin. Then her imagination turns to selecting clothes from her sumptuous wardrobe to enhance these items. This daydreaming gives her pleasure, particularly when she spots the elderly gentleman again strolling around the store.

He's dapperly dressed in a close-fitting, shimmering satin suit, the color of which seems to change from blue to a pink depending upon the lights surrounding him. His features, too, seem to change according to the dominating tone.

How strange, Gabrielle thinks. If the manager didn't know his name, I'd believe he's some superhuman being, a visitor to this earth. Why is he being so generous to me? I've almost taken his second gift for granted, and I seem to be expecting a third one. But, then again, I did ask Natas for a luxurious life.

"You're lost in thought," a gentle voice murmurs behind her.

"I guess so," Gabrielle answers, turning around. "I've been wondering when you would appear again."

"So, you've gotten accustomed to being given to and admired?" he asks, looking lovingly at her.

"I guess so," she responds, flustered. She reaches into the counter bin ready to show him her next selection. He apologizes for being abrupt and, as suddenly, disappears.

The manager—who has been observing the entire scene—approaches Gabrielle, asking heatedly if she has offended Mr. Jiran.

"I haven't, have you?" she bounces back at him. "Shouldn't you be paying more attention to store business rather than being a watchdog over mine?"

He gallops away infuriated, and Gabrielle tells herself, nice work, but you've really got an enemy now! He will be a foe as long as I have the jewelry. Why did Mr. Jiran leave? He'll be back. Am I being too sure of myself? No. I just know he will, and it will be at the right time.

At the closing of the store, she goes to place her jewels in her safety deposit box. An eerie feeling overtakes her while she dials the combination to open the box. Sensing someone behind her, she deliberately dials the wrong number. When she feels she is again alone, she dials the right combination. Okay, store manager, you don't know what you're in for, she declares in silence.

When she exits the store, she notices a pink stretch limousine in front of it. Mr. Jiran waves to her from his car window, and Gabrielle waves back, watching the extraordinary vehicle disappear into the traffic.

Her manager is standing behind her, so Gabrielle rushes into a crowd of people and disappears into a subway. He's dangerous, she thinks on her way to her apartment.

At home, she turns on the television, which happens to be showing a film starring Jesse Jason. Gabrielle, astonished, wonders what destiny is trying to tell her. Shall I watch it or shall I play it safe and protect my feelings? Gabrielle decides to watch the film. Through this serendipitous turn of events, she gains another perspective about Jesse: his looks, his talent, his appeal. I'm still attracted to you, but I know from experience that you're a pathetic man, she acknowledges to herself.

With that realization, she turns off the television and fantasizes about Mr. Jiran. He's older than me. That's okay, he'll be kind and I won't have to worry about money. What would life be like married to him? I'd live in a mansion, wear gorgeous clothes, meet interesting people, travel the world, and even have a baby. Even though he's older, a baby would be wonderful because I'd have a lot of help. I'd teach Mr. Jiran how to love and vice versa. Hmmm, what would love feel like? So good, so awfully good—secure, everlasting—no demands, except to love him and cherish him. I could do that even though he's not handsome like Jesse or as virile. Hey, wake up, Gabrielle, be in reality: You have a rotten past. You're in the store because of Natas. Would such an elegant gentleman want a whore like you?

She pinches herself and placates her nature with it makes him feel good to give jewelry to a clerk in a store—that's all. Wake up. She assures herself of her rationale, but leaves room for doubt.

The next morning when she opens the safety deposit box, she notices finger marks on the handles. She opens it with trepidation, but she finds all of the contents intact. Wearing all of her jewelry, she walks toward her counter. Awaiting her is Mr. Jiran, who tells her playfully,

"I beat you here this morning, heavenly angel."

"You did," responds Gabrielle, astonished yet pleased. "You're an early riser, I notice."

"Sometimes. I want you to show me what you have in mind," he tells her.

"But…but…how do you know?"

"Never mind, I just do," he replies and laughs politely as he gazes at her with longing. Gabrielle's face flushes scarlet. "Too much too soon, my dear? In time you'll get used to it—and even more." Gabrielle wants to hide inside one of her bins but finds herself swaying back and forth as though she will faint.

"Take my hand to steady you. There now, focus on me—that's right. You're steadier now? Good, now show me what you have in mind."

"All right." More grounded, Gabrielle reaches for the gems: a pair of earrings and a bracelet. She puts them on; Mr. Jiran steps back and beholds her as though seeing a glittering star in heaven. He invites all in the store to look at the amazing vision. Gabrielle soaks in the adoration, his generosity, and his love, while at the same time she pushes away the black, glaring energy of the manager from the far corner of the store.

Mr. Jiran writes his check, this time for the largest sum of money ever. Before he leaves, he asks, "Dinner tomorrow night, after work? Wear all I've given you. The limousine will be outside."

Gabrielle nods weakly, overwhelmed and yet joyous. He leaves, but this time he turns around near the entrance of the store and waves to her. She lifts her hand and waves back, managing a sweet smile filled with wonder at what's happening to her. The manager, on the other hand, is perplexed, takes the check that Gabrielle absentmindedly hands him, and becomes invisible for the rest of the day.

Gabrielle spends that day wondering about Mr. Jiran. Who is he? Why does he have such a powerful effect on me, powerful enough for me to become dizzy and almost faint? I wish we could meet tonight instead of waiting until tomorrow.

❦

When the next day's work is finished, Gabrielle rushes to the ladies' room and puts fresh makeup on her face. She changes from her suit into an exquisite dress with accompanying accessories and rearranges her jewelry. Finally she steps in front of a tall mirror and exclaims, "Wow, Gabrielle, you are beautiful. You're just beginning to accept this fact." She's beaming as she leaves the ladies' room, unexpectedly stumbling upon the manager, who greets her and asks whether she needs help putting her jewelry away. "No thanks," she tells him as she brushes by.

He protests, "But, but, you're not wearing all those gems home, are you? Didn't you tell me it wouldn't be safe?"

"I said no," Gabrielle retorts, pushing him out of her way; and she rushes through the entrance of the store, which is monitored by a store policeman.

Mr. Jiran is standing at his limousine, and he extends his hand to help her jump into the pink limousine. Mr. Jiran gives the manager, standing in the entrance, a cursory salute and enters the car. The manager stands with his mouth hanging open—dumbfounded and totally defeated.

Gabrielle's exasperation from her encounter with her enemy compels her to explain the complicated story to Mr. Jiran. He listens attentively as the limousine pushes its way through the dense city traffic. She continues talking about her supervisor all the way to the elegant restaurant Mr. Jiran has chosen.

In their private dining room, Gabrielle's excitement escalates, and Mr. Jiran continues to listen, mesmerized by her humanness and innocence. His sparkling eyes keep prodding her to reveal more and more about herself. Never having had so much attention, kindness, and caring, Gabrielle responds from a soul level, engaged completely from her real self. She's lost in amazement that another person finds her fascinating and that the story of her life keeps him riveted.

"Come home with me, Gabrielle. We'll have an after-dinner drink." She consents, and right after they arrive, he shows her every room in his luxurious four-story mansion.

She is stunned. "Do you live here alone?" she finally asks.

"All alone, Gabrielle, except for the servants. I'm looking for the right mate."

"Oh," replies Gabrielle. After sipping her crème de cacao and many minutes have passed she tells him, "I must go now, but I can't take the jewels with me because of the neighborhood I live in."

"Then stay here overnight and my chauffeur will take you to the store in the morning. There is only one condition."

Her heart sinks. "What is that?"

"On the condition we'll do this again soon. Next time we'll eat here."

"I'd like that."

He shows her to a guest room, where he kisses her on her forehead and bids her goodnight. Gabrielle sleeps soundly, wondering whether she has embarked on a fairytale journey. She savors all of it: a perfumed bath drawn by a servant in the morning, and then being shown a wardrobe of clothing from which she selects an appropriate suit for the store. Next, she is ushered into a dining room where one of Mr. Jiran's butlers serves her breakfast, explaining, "Mr. Jiran had to be out early on a business call. He apologizes."

She wears all of her jewelry and is whisked off to the store in a white limousine. "Mr. Jiran's apologizes for the white limousine. He took the pink one," mutters the driver.

He has *two* limousines, she ponders, her head spinning until suddenly she finds herself in the familiarity of the entrance to the store.

The store is cordoned off by a police squadron, and an ambulance is standing in the midst of the police cars. A crowd of people has gathered behind the ropes, peering intently to determine the reasons for the restrictions. Gabrielle rushes to the store's police guard, and at the same moment, several ambulance attendants pass by with the manager's body on a stretcher. His eyes are rolled to the top of his sockets, and he's mumbling incoherently.

"What happened?" Gabrielle screams.

The guard replies, "He was trapped in the store's huge safe since last night. The lock of the safe jammed, and he's been stuck inside: it's a miracle he's still breathing. The night watchman heard him bang weakly on the safe door earlier this morning. He called the owner and locksmiths, the cops, and the hospital. What chaos until they all got here! And he looks like a ghost. I hope they can revive him; he's really close to death. But, you know, he's a peculiar man—you never know what's on his mind."

Once inside the store, Gabrielle runs to her safe deposit box and notices that it was tampered with again. I can get the police to photograph the fingerprints, she thinks. But I won't. He's learned his lesson, and maybe he won't be back for a while. That's a horrible accident to endure. Strange that I told Mr. Jiran about his weird behavior just last night and then this happens. She feels ill at ease, but she shrugs off the feeling with the thought that we reap what we sow. The day moves slowly, and Gabrielle is anxious to leave the store.

Back at her apartment, Gabrielle recalls in detail and with great pleasure the adventure with Mr. Jiran. Well, I told him a lot about myself, everything except that I'm a call girl. Maybe that'll be next. I don't want to lie to someone who is so kind to me. But that might well be the *coup de grace*. But, maybe not.

She turns on the television and again is confronted by an earlier film of Jesse's. You again, she thinks as she watches it. You're not kind and generous like Mr. Jiran. I believe he truly cares for me, unless he's acting. No, you are the one who puts on an act, Jesse, not him. How different I feel when I'm with him than when I was with you. Your heart's in a straitjacket. Of what use is it to think about us? None. It's a waste of time.

She turns off the television. I'd like to be in Mr. Jiran's company right now; it's so satisfying—I turn into a vivacious, wondering, imaginative child, which feels so good. It feels good because it's a true part of me, the part that never had an outlet when I was growing up. I believe I could be nurtured this way for the rest of my life. Would I get tired of it? Right now, that seems far-fetched. How can you get tired of being cared for, appreciated, and loved? Gabrielle reflects on this question and is convinced a million years would go by before she'd get bored. With that, she smiles contentedly and calls for Natas.

When Natas appears, Gabrielle recounts all that has transpired. She becomes aware of how similarly she speaks to both Natas and

Mr. Jiran. They're both good listeners, she observes, and I need that attention—there's nothing wrong with that.

Natas sniffs, grunts and snorts as it listens. "What do you want from me, Gabrielle?"

"I don't know, Natas, except that I want Mr. Jiran to propose to me. I want a different kind of life."

"You do? Well, well, and in such a short time of knowing him. Well, well." It disappears.

At the store, Gabrielle is greeted by a new manager, who hands her a sealed envelope. She opens it and reads the enclosed note written on handsome notepaper:

> *Dear Gabrielle, heavenly angel:*
>
> *My business calls me away for a week,*
> *but when I return, let's have dinner at my home. As a matter*
> *of fact, I propose a specific time—next Wednesday, after your*
> *work. My chauffeur will be waiting outside the store without*
> *my presence because I will be attending to the culinary chores. I*
> *await your presence with great anticipation.*
>
> *Your friend and...*
>
> *Mr. Jiran*

The magic time, Wednesday, arrives at last. Gabrielle has been counting the days as well as the hours. The store no longer interests her—what does interest her are Mr. Jiran and the love he so generously bestows upon her.

When the limousine reaches his home, Mr. Jiran is standing outside of his door, an apron wrapped around his waist. He opens the car door and out steps the alluring Gabrielle, excited and happy to see him. He folds her into his arms, holding her tightly against his body. She feels him gasp for breath as she gyrates slightly with her pelvis against his. Rather than respond, he gets flustered, takes her by the hand, and ushers her into his home.

Gabrielle is beaming, ready to tell him how much she missed their meetings. But, once inside, he holds her away from him, to sing his adoring praises to her beauty. Gabrielle, ecstatic, is ready to climb all over his body until the heat of their feelings would tell them what to do next. He, though, is restrained with an agenda that extinguishes the fire between them. So, she, too, holds back her impulses.

He takes her into the kitchen where the aroma of cooking catches her interest. She exuberantly goes to the stove, lifts the covers off the pots, and savors all he and the cook are making. Mr. Jiran tells her to call him by his first name, Gamiel. "I will," says Gabrielle. "It's an unusual name."

"Yes and no," Gamiel replies. "Let's go into the dining room where our drinks are ready." Gabrielle holds his hand, which is ice cold. She asks teasingly whether he spent the week in the Arctic. Unsettled, he responds, "No, just a sign of excitement." Gabrielle contemplates: Excitement is hot, not cold. But, okay.

He toasts her, again calling her his heavenly angel. She toasts him in return saying, "Gamiel, my savior." He turns scarlet. During their meal, Gabrielle requests he be more forthcoming about his life. "You know, the last time we were together, I told you almost everything there is to know about me. You're reserved speaking about your own life. Why?"

"Because you're more interesting, Gabrielle, he responds sincerely. "I'm an ordinary man with a sordid past—not too interesting."

"Your past is sordid?" she exclaims.

"I'm a fisher of humanity—lost humanity. I do business with them if they let me. If they don't we go our separate ways. But, invariably they call me back. And when I return, they pay a price. Everything in life has a price, isn't that true, Gabrielle?"

Gabrielle listens intently trying to understand what he is really meaning. "That's true, Gamiel, there's always a price that we pay if our lives are unprincipled."

"Waywardness, weakness, lostness are the ingredients—among many other qualities—from which my business flourishes. I am not a nice person, Gabrielle. You're the only one I've ever adored and given to. That's the truth. And my feelings for you often cause me remorse about my life. Perhaps you can save me."

Gabrielle sits quietly while she listens, eating little and considering, oh, dear, this smacks of having to take care of someone again. But she corrects herself, that's not true, the others gave nothing back—Gamiel is more than generous. Why so much mystery, though? I suppose he'll talk more when he's ready. And with that thought she resumes eating.

"I love your attentiveness, Gabrielle," Gamiel continues. "Yes, I too have needs—many." He is quiet, as though reflecting on what he is admitting. "I won't burden you with them all at once. In time, you'll know who I truly am. And now for our after-dinner drink. Would I be presumptuous to assume that you are not going home tonight? Your room is waiting for you."

Gabrielle is delighted and nods yes like a child to his question.

"And, of course we'll do the same thing tomorrow night after your work is finished. Are you in agreement?"

"Yes," Gabrielle agrees, goes to Gamiel, and kisses him lightly on his lips. He gasps again, but moves away from her while he shows her to her room. In parting, Gamiel tells her, "I delight in you."

"I do, too—in you," Gabrielle tells him, and they part.

Gabrielle pushes all doubts, questions, and reservations away from her brain. Instead she enjoys the emerging of details in each moment. Again, he is not at breakfast, but that doesn't matter. She eats breakfast in the company of the butler.

When the chauffeur drops her off at the store, his only comment is, "The same time as last night, Miss Gabrielle?"

"The same time, Robert."

She bids the new manager good morning, goes to her counter, and resumes the day, waiting impatiently for the evening with Gamiel.

Her workday ended, as before he awaits her arrival outside. They greet each other with a tight hug—their genitals touching longer, until he pulls himself away, uncontrollably excited. Gabrielle, like a chirping bird, begins talking about the happenings of the day. Gamiel finds her chirping charming and desirable, and he listens to every word. Their evening is spent in the dining room—talking and experiencing the blossoming love they have for one another.

Gabrielle goes to her room as usual, but Gamiel lingers longer at the threshold. "I need you to hold me, Gabrielle, strongly." As she does so, he whispers, "More—more. Oh, it's so good." He kisses her on her lips, gasps—and darts away.

Wow! Little by little, Gabrielle exclaims silently. She sleeps soundly.

The next morning Gamiel is in the kitchen with a readied breakfast for both of them. "You'll be here tonight, Gabrielle?" he asks timidly. "And the next night as well?" She nods and kisses him lightly on the lips and speeds to work.

❦

One day becomes interwoven with the next, their feelings growing in intensity as well as evolving into intimacy. After a week of Gamiel's rushing away on the threshold of her room, he asks with trepidation, "May I come in, Gabrielle?"

She is taken aback but nods her guileless nod.

"Don't turn on the light, Gabrielle," Gamiel requests adamantly. "Don't ever turn on the light! Promise?"

"Yes, Gamiel."

His naked body slips into bed beside hers. "Oh, oh, oh, my beloved," he whispers. "Oh, let me caress you all over as I've wanted to do from the beginning."

"Do so, Gamiel," whispers Gabrielle soothingly. She is astonished at his tentativeness and gentleness.

"Oh, Gabrielle, my Gabrielle," he continues whispering, his desire escalating, "it's all new to me. Help me with your pleasure and mine as well. She does. They lie intertwined, his body still vibrating from passion. And then he slips out of the bed. "Goodnight, my love." He leaves.

Gabrielle is too astonished to think, and she sleeps fretfully. He is not at breakfast the next morning, nor for the rest of the week. His note tells her to make his home hers and never again to go to her

51

apartment—he will return soon. When she questions her driver about where Mr. Jiran has gone, his response is, "I don't know. It's always like this. Really, nobody knows—we just await his return. So should you."

❧

Gabrielle has now been living in Mr. Jiran's mansion for two months. Their lovemaking in the dark becomes more intense for both of them. Gamiel is ecstatic, wanting Gabrielle the moment he lays eyes on her. She, too, enjoys him even though she takes the role of an aggressive partner.

All of their amorous activity continues to take place in the dark, with his departure shortly after their lovemaking has ended. Gabrielle wonders how a man of his age can be so innocent and yet so passionate at the same time. Along with it all, she enjoys the surroundings—even the rhythm of going to work and returning to Gamiel in the evenings. His adoration of her is so intense that it sometimes frightens her. Gabrielle, however, is being healed of her early deprivation.

❧

In the two months of her stay with Gamiel, she notices that her menstrual flow has ceased, which has her perturbed. 'Is it possible that I'm pregnant?' she wonders. I would want a baby, but it's too soon. We're just getting acquainted, and there are so many unexplainable things about him. If I am pregnant, then I must tell him, but I'm reluctant to do so. He's so sensitive, unworldly and in some ways unpredictable. However, if I can't be honest with him, what kind of relationship will we have? I'll tell him tonight.

Her resolve is made, but when he lays his eyes on her, he is compelled to take Gabrielle into her room. He pushes her onto the bed, tears off her clothing, and ravages her, shouting and moaning, "Oh, God, God, God—it's so good, I never dreamed it could be so good. It's you, Gabrielle, who makes me feel this way, you and only you. Oh, God! How I love you, beautiful Gabrielle, Gabrielle of my dreams, my heart, my life." He finally crumbles to her side and weeps bitterly. "Why wasn't I open to this ecstasy before? Oh, my God, why did you allow me to forsake you? Is this your punishment for my horrible pride? I haven't spoken to you for eons. Are you listening to me, are you laughing at me? No, no, that would be something *I* would be capable of."

He turns to Gabrielle in the dark and asks, "Are you there? Do you hear my crazy mumbling? Are you a witch who has cast a spell on me? Oh, Gabrielle, I want you again." He mounts her body, this time needing no help, no stimulation from her. And he loves her with a passion that stuns even Gabrielle. "We're one, aren't we, Gabrielle? That's what all this lovemaking is about, isn't it—we're one, never to be apart?"

"Yes, Gamiel," whispers Gabrielle ecstatically. "You're such a passionate lover, and you satisfy me completely."

"There will never be another? No Jesse Jason?" he asks bordering on hysteria.

"No one but you for eternity," Gabrielle calmly assures him.

"Oh, my Gabrielle," he whispers as he lies contentedly on his back next to her, his partner.

The sun is rising slowly, and at that moment Gamiel reluctantly pushes himself away from her side and unwillingly leaves the room. Silently watching, Gabrielle notices that as he opens the bedroom door, a pink hue pervades the walls, the floor, and the furniture. It must be the sun's rays reflected in the room, she supposes. Well, she thinks, this wasn't the right time to tell him. I'll wait for a more appropriate moment. She sleeps as though she had been shipwrecked.

The next morning, she arrives at the store and the manager requests that she change her jewelry. "They're no longer items of variety and interest," he explains to her. "Here are other jewels that will keep the public interested. Place your own into the safety deposit box, and we'll see how these will do attracting new customers." Gabrielle agrees and wears the new selection of adornments.

One evening, however, she forgets to exchange them for Gamiel's. She arrives at his mansion, and he is in the kitchen happily cooking her favorite dishes. When she walks into the kitchen, he turns toward her and notices the new gems. He is too astonished to say anything.

At dinner, Gabrielle notices his distancing and questions him whether something is wrong. He avoids the question and almost hisses at her. Wishing to have their usual closeness, Gabrielle sits on a sofa and places his hand on her belly. He's unclear about her gesture and quickly removes his hand. She repeats her gesture. "Gamiel," she pleads, "whatever is bothering you should be talked about."

He almost snarls at her, "Those jewels, who gave them to you? She explains until he understands. Finally he responds, "My jealousy—you're mine; nobody else's?"

"Yes," says Gabrielle, wondering whether he is always paranoid or whether it is a passing phase in their relationship. She takes a deep breath and replies patiently, "I'm yours and to prove it, I have your seed in my womb, your child. Haven't you noticed how much fuller my abdomen is these days?"

She notices the idea slowly penetrating his brain. After a few moments, he places his hand on her abdomen. "My seed, Gabrielle?"

"Yours, Gamiel."

He is in awe. He sits beside Gabrielle and kisses her hands and face, overcome by an array of feelings gushing forth at once. Then he lifts her off the sofa and carries her into her room, where his ardor erupts like no other time. He sings praises to her, to her womb, to God, to the universe. His restraints have vanished, and Gabrielle is inundated by his all-encompassing love.

Gamiel, finding a new glory about life, fantasizes to himself, his brain racing: I hope that the baby is good-looking like me, Gamiel, but most important that it looks like Gabrielle. Of course it will be a boy. If it is a girl, I would like that too. How will I raise it? I know nothing about children. Gabrielle will do the raising since I'm away so much. It will work out. My child? Oh, my God!

The sun is streaming daylight through the windows into the room. Unaware that the darkness has turned into light, Gamiel forgets to leave the bed and continues his exciting thoughts. Because he is unusually quiet, Gabrielle reaches her hand out to her partner, to stroke his skin, to caress him. She hears a sniffing, snorting, hissing response. Both Gabrielle and Gamiel are astounded. Gamiel touches himself to feel the coarseness of his skin and the size of his head; and when he looks down at his body, he realizes it is pink all over. He tries to sneak out of the room, but the sun is fully present—and when he turns to Gabrielle, she is facing him on her knees, bewildered and shocked.

"You're Natas, not Gamiel. What have you done with Gamiel?" she shrieks. "Bring him back! I want *him*, not *you*. Bring him back. I love him, not you!" She sobs uncontrollably.

"Oh, Gabrielle, I forgot to leave because I love you so much." It reaches toward her, but Gabrielle recoils from its touch. "Why? Why Natas, why did you betray me?"

"I love you, Gabrielle," it pleads with her. "I want so much to be normal, but God doesn't want that for me. I was learning to be a good man—you're responsible for that."

"What about me? I love Gamiel so deeply and want to have his baby. Now what shall I do? Is it going to look like you, be like you—divided, sordid?" Gabrielle sobs hysterically, her body folded over her knees, her head buried in a pillow. She whimpers pathetically, "I've never gotten it right, but this is the most horrific mistake I've ever made. 'Turn yourself back into Gamiel so that I can believe in you again—*please!"*

Natas leaves the room in remorse, telling her that he must make an alchemical change, the secret of which is known only to God and to him. In an hour's time, he returns as Gamiel—but the nature of Natas still pervades him.

Gabrielle looks at Gamiel in disgust, leaves her bed, and she forlornly gathers her belongings into a suitcase, ready to leave the mansion. Gamiel—hoping to persuade her to stay—is standing at the front entry, passive, bereft, and mute.

For the last time, Gabrielle is driven to the store by Robert in one of the limousines. But she is too distraught to work, so she feigns illness and prepares herself to return to her apartment with Gamiel's jewelry safely tucked away in the bottom of her purse.

❧

She walks away from the store like a sleepwalker, her disappointment and bewilderment etched deeply into her face. A few blocks from the jewelry store, Gabrielle notices a handsome but shabbily-clothed, blond man in slippered feet, sitting on the sidewalk of a commercial building. He is holding up a handwritten sign with the words:

PLEASE HELP.
ANYTHING WILL DO.

She recognizes the person is Jesse Jason. Even though she is in deep despair, she fumbles in her purse for two easily accessible earrings she had worn the night before and drops them into his cup. And as she does that, she briefly asks him, "Natas?" He nods. "Thanks for the earrings. They'll help."

She continues her walk to her apartment, feeling less sorry for herself after seeing how Jesse has ended up. But when she arrives at her entry door, she finds it bolted with a **NO TRESPASSING** sign plastered over it. She had forgotten to pay the rent while she was staying with Gamiel.

She opens her purse looking for coins to call a hotel to house her for the day. As she sticks her hand into the bottom of her handbag she finds that the jewels she had carefully placed there had melted into outlines of what they were. She is penniless. "You can't sustain fairness and honesty instead of vindictiveness and hatred for any length of time without my presence, can you, Natas?" she rages at the creature.

Her job at the store continues and her pregnancy is an enhancement attracting many women in the same condition to her counter. Their husbands are enchanted and buy lavishly for their expecting wives, inspired by Gabrielle's beauty and her pregnancy. From time to time Gabrielle notices Gamiel lurking outside the store's display window looking at her longingly; but he never dares to enter, and people do not inquire about him.

❧

One day, her five-month pregnancy has repercussions on Gabrielle's body. She is seized with severe abdominal pain and is taken to the emergency room of a nearby hospital. In a short period of time, she miscarries. Although the contractions are excruciating, Gabrielle is relieved of her persistent, gnawing fear that the child would resemble Natas.

When she emerges from the anesthesia after her D & C surgery, she casually asks her nurse what the fetus looked like. At first, the nurse is reluctant to tell her, but since Gabrielle is so inquisitive, she explains, "It was the weirdest creation I ever saw. It was pink all over—not like human pigment but as though someone had sprayed the body with a can of pink paint. It had a huge head that already had teeth in its mouth. I thought at first it was a reptile of sorts. I could have sworn that it was hissing. But, I have a vivid imagination. It was a boy."

Gabrielle remains silent which encourages the nurse to continue, "You know, in the beginning of a fetus' life, God's creatures take strange forms before they mature into humans. So, you shouldn't feel bad about the description I'm giving you." She stops for a moment wondering if she'd gone too far. "Are you all right now that you're back to normal? Any regrets?" she asks, looking at Gabrielle strangely.

"I won't have a baby and that's unfortunate," she replies after much thought, "but sometimes miscarriages are best for the fetus and the mother—so I'd say it's a blessing."

The nurse smiles and leaves, impressed by Gabrielle's intelligent approach to the matter; she is now certain she was right to be as forthright as she was.

Gabrielle thanks her and smiles back. Her smile is forced, however, what with so many other feelings swimming around in her heart. She reasons, I can still smile. That's a good sign. I'm not totally destroyed. She breathes deeply feeling her body from her head to her feet. She gives silent praise and gratitude for her empty womb—devoid of a could-have-been Natas.

"Okay, God, that was a horrendous ordeal. We humans learn—but barely. What's next?"

PART 2

THE CONCEPTS UNDERNEATH THE STORY

INTRODUCTION

Gabrielle said: "Okay, God, that was a horrendous ordeal. We humans learn—but barely. What's next?"

I say: "We humans learn, but barely—until our consciousness changes and the eyes of God look out from inside our souls to recognize that what's next is to tackle another piece of the puzzle: the parental demonic voices as well as Satan's. Both voices have the Father of Lies as their origin, and both are huge obstacles in the way of completing our earthly mission.

"What's next? What's next?!" pleads Gabrielle as she once again sits by the pond after her hospital experience. This body of water had become a place of quiet and introspection for her. She was listening— listening to what, she didn't know. But as she listened, she heard:

> *Rid yourself of the darkness.*
> *Come into the light of God's*
> *love. Beg God to give you*
> *insight and wisdom to overcome*
> *these forces. Start with your own*
> *infiltrated psyche, then look at your*
> *neighbor's, then beyond. Be ecstatic*
> *that you are doing this for yourself*
> *first, then the neighbor's, then beyond.*
> *Thus the world will be swept clean.*

"Who are you, Natas? Who are you, Satan?" Gabrielle screams to the ripples on the water of the pond. The answers come.

CHAPTER 1
EXPOSING SATAN

WHAT IS THE SATANIC ENERGY?

In this world, man's inhumanity to man, his irrational behavior toward man, his schizophrenic lack of feeling, and his mindless cruelty are rampant. In New York City, a young person was pushed in front of a subway train by an assailant who had no conscious motive other than what his voices told him to do. The hand of the victim, a violinist, was severed from her wrist. Or take, for example, a young mother who doused her constantly screaming baby with boiling water and then placed it into a lit gas oven to release the Devil from his soul. When the husband arrived, the baby was beyond help. Countless individuals suffer at the hands of those who torture, kill, maim, and destroy with little or no conscience. What accounts for such behavior?

Even those who are considered outstanding examples of virtue struggle with evil in themselves. St. Paul wrote:

> *For what I do is not the good I want to do;*
> *no, the evil I do not want to do—this I keep*
> *on doing. Now if I do what I do not want*
> *to do, it is no longer I who do it, but it is*
> *sin living in me that does it.*

(Romans 7: 19-20)

He, too, was enslaved: A war waged between his demons and his love for the Holy Spirit. St. Paul represents the human being's struggle between the darkness and the light. All human beings wage this war. It is when we do not recognize the dark forces in our psyches that they become powerful.

Philip, the author of the Gospel of Philip, which was found at Nag Hammadi in 1945, advises the reader:

> *...let each of us dig down to the root*
> *of evil within us, and pull out the root*
> *from the heart. It will be plucked out if*
> *we recognize it. But if we do not*
> *recognize it, it takes root in our hearts*
> *and produces its fruits in our hearts.*
> *It masters us, and makes us its slaves.*

—cf Gospel of Philip, NHC 11, 3, 74.5-12

But what exactly is that root of evil? Where did it come from? And how do we pluck it out? We will remain slaves until we understand exactly what—or who—we have become enslaved by.

Theologians have written and argued endlessly throughout theological history about the story of two angels defecting from heaven at the beginning of time on Earth. The first to defect was Lucifer, who—because of God's seeming preference for his younger offspring, God's first human creation, Adam—fell from heaven through pride and envy. Lucifer's love turned into hatred, and Lucifer threatened to take up its throne against God and to divide the universe. Making good on its threat, Lucifer became the personification of sin and the lord of fornication, war, bloodshed, exile, death, panic, and destruction. It took a horde of angels with it.

The second angel to defect was Samyaza, who developed an insatiable lust for the daughters of men upon Earth and to beget children by them. Samyaza convinced two hundred angels called Watchers to join its mission. The women they coupled with gave birth to giants whose appetites could not be satiated. In time, these giants turned their needs on *homo sapiens*, literally consuming them as food. God's wrath resounded in the heavens, as God claimed that angels are of the spirit and cannot mingle with the dense matter of earth inhabitants. Nine-tenths of the angels were condemned to the underworld and were never again able to have access to God or his domain.

Certain scholars believe that one-tenth of these angels still exist in our world—influencing its politics, its society, its culture, and its people. Since the Watchers' credo denies the sovereignty of God, they will seek out the righteous to entrap or slay them. Bound to Earth by God's judgment as long as the world endures, the Watchers create havoc to this day, affecting the planet and all humankind. God's judgment proclaims that they shall remain as evil spirits upon Earth and they will never obtain peace.[4]

Their effects are multifarious, creating patterns of behavior in the psyche of humanity that can explain its stuckness, its inability to seek wholeness—and at the extreme end of the spectrum, what we call "human" cruelty. These sinister patterns are manifested by Lucifer and its followers; they are master puppeteers, and until we discover how to contend with them, we are their victims.

Thus they are a force that needs to be recognized, challenged, and fought by humanity, particularly when our quest is to seek the wisdom of God and to listen to God's voice at all times. Is it not ironic that not only do we have to undo the aberrations of our parents and of society in general, but we also have to be discerning about Lucifer and its "gang" *and* the Watchers' infiltration into our psyches? Life on this Earth is a full undertaking, to be dealt with seriously and to be valued as an important experience on the way not only to healing but to becoming a whole being.

HOW WE FALL PREY TO SATAN

Satan exists. Its passion is to destroy, to obliterate, and to possess any vestige of reason, sanity, and desire for our *I* and our *I Am* identities. We, the recipients of such malice, develop and nurture the ingredients for its infestation because of our indulgences. Why? Because we have fallen from Grace.

We, like Lucifer, have felt irrationally rejected by God because we are not his only love. On numerous occasions, I regressed my patients to the beginnings of their creation. All of these sessions revealed a common denominator: Each patient reported leaving God's heaven, reluctantly blaming God for casting them out. And forever after, like Lucifer, they blamed the Deity for ostracizing them. This separation resulted in human sin, making the chasm between God and his children almost irreparable.

As one patient said in her hypnotic trance:

> I followed him, like a child.
> I was always under him,
> around him, on top,
> inside, outside.
> Sometimes God tripped and
> fell over me.
> I whined:
> "I want to be like you."
>
> He said:
> *"You are you. Be you.*
> *I am who I am.*
> *You are who you are. Be it."*
>
> And then he said most gently:
> *"Get out from under my feet, or*
> *I will blow you out of heaven."*
>
> I heard, but did not listen.
>
> The war began.
> Not his—mine.
> And mine alone.
> "You don't want me?
> I'll fight you all the way.
> You are no longer my God!"

Whether or not the above experience is the product of my patient's rich imagination, it is a believable metaphor that can spark us to understand the age-old concept: As above, so below. When we descend from heaven and are filled with rage at God, our souls become easy fodder for the evil forces. Isn't God Satan's worst enemy? In our efforts to justify our rage and our separation from the Divinity, we can become undefined, hateful creatures steeped in Earth's ways—disconnected from ourselves and from his teachings of wisdom, love, humility, and honesty. Our heavenly, protective shield is dissociated. We intuitively feel alone, and this aloneness is an elixir for the forces of evil. Their evil proliferates as our susceptibilities to their evil germinate.

In my second book, *Rage at God: Ascending to Reunion,*[5] I explain that just like Lucifer, many people have feelings of rage toward God and therefore are incapable of connecting to the Deity in a true way. Further, they cannot have a direct experience of God that is not in some way distorted by the relationship with their own parents. The rage at the mother or the father, as an authority, becomes rage toward God. For example, when I asked a patient in my practice—who mouthed the word "God" as though she were chewing tobacco—about her real feelings toward the Divinity, she was at a loss to understand her ambivalence. I directed her to visualize God on the right side of her body and her father on the left side. With no hesitation, she screamed at Jesus, "You alcoholic zombie—get off those two sticks, come down, and take care of me!" She was speaking to her perpetually drunk earthly father, unconsciously equating him with the Divinity. This type of parental transference onto God, I have discovered, is commonplace.

Without this realization, she might have continued her disconnection to God, remaining cut off from her Source. It might have been only a short period of disconnection or it could have taken centuries before a meaningful illumination became possible. Like Lucifer, all of us might be consumed by venomous rage toward Father/Mother God for eons of time.

Separation from God and deviation from God's covenant lead to darkness. Our journey in life then becomes a walk in an unlit labyrinth. But—we always have choices.

FREE WILL
Free will has been ordained by God and is a necessary ingredient for human development. Renowned psychoanalyst, Dr. Eric Fromm, claims *that we are not created evil or forced to be evil, but we become evil slowly over time through a long series of choices.*[6] Through free choice, the being defines himself or herself. The soul stands by, desirous to be heard,

but when the self is separated not only from its soul but from God, it is mastered by its own will, not the Will of God. The being has lost the realization that the soul and God monitor its life. The self is thus often thrust back for centuries to remain in its maze.

Free will can thus lend itself to satanic infiltration. If the soul defects from her heavenly home with rage at God or other disgruntlements, she will become bound to a *Not I* credo, which will estrange her from God's heaven and make her prey to Satan and its cohorts. An example of such rage at God was given above. As has been said without equivocation by M. Scott Peck, M.D., a world-renowned psychiatrist:

> There are only two states of being:
> submission to God and goodness
> or the refusal to submit to anything
> beyond one's own will—which
> refusal automatically enslaves one
> to the forces of evil. [7]

I am in agreement with Dr. Peck, and I vouch for the fact that willfulness leads to misdeeds. These misdeeds create partners in crime—one misdeed paving the way to the next—not unlike the alcoholic in a saloon who is invited by other alcoholics to "have another drink for the road." The trap is set. The susceptible one falls into the trap. Satan, the hunter, bamboozles its new acquisitions. It wants the destruction of human beings, and human beings listening to the forces of evil will soon succumb.

The circle begins its repetitive motion. "What was done to me, I'll do to you," says the parent to the offspring. "I never had it any better, so, why should you?" Or, "Isn't the Jesus of the Bible known to have drunk a lot of wine while he was on Earth? Do you want to be a follower? Then go all the way!" The evil ones are masters of deceit.

PATTERNS

Free will enables us to lie to ourselves if we choose to. When we make that choice, patterns ripe with satanic influence begin to form instantly. When these are not seriously addressed, we end up tucking them away, consciously or unconsciously, in a subterranean vault in our psyche. We secretly hope that the patterns will never be seen or heard from again. We have then fallen into a state of laziness and indulgence, shifting out of reality—and onto the dangerous road to satanic infiltration.

A dramatic example of such a state is that of fifty-year-old Bill, one of my patients, who consistently used his extensive knowledge of psychology to manipulate those around him. Another patient, a woman who was befuddled by Bill's explanation about why he had lost yet another job, said of him, "He's a real conundrum." We become conundrums when the dark forces take over.

Bill's explanation, spoken with confidence and clarity, lulled the listener into believing his fantasies, illusions, and psychological logic. But one day during a group session, the real reason for his job loss was exposed: As a child, he had made an ironclad decision not to be self-sufficient. To punish his parents for their abusive behavior toward him, he had decided that he would always be taken care of. When this early resolve was exposed, he sat before us naked, a fish caught in a net. He then tried his most effective ploy, a very serious one for me as well as for his listeners—the threat of suicide. His bluff was called. No one flinched. He eventually backed off, mouthing, "I got the attention I wanted, didn't I?"

This pattern had worked for him all of his life with his family; they had become his pawns. Little did Bill or his family realize that all of them—including Bill—had become the slaves of an eminently more skillful and dangerous enemy: Satan.

Bill's inner rationalized thinking can sound something like this:

> No one will know, no one will see.
> Do I have to look at everything?
> I'm sure they're my secrets only.
> I'll get others' help with them.
> They'll be glad to give me the support I need.
> It'll make them feel good.
> It'll take the pressure off the truth.
> Too tired. Too busy. Besides,
> God's too busy to pay attention to
> insignificant me.

Such droning thoughts are satanic. If only we were aware…but we choose to ignore the pattern and we choose to not hear clearly. Consequently, the patterns and the voices accumulate and re-form their energies until a person becomes dulled to their existence, yet is guided and lives by them.

Another patient, Janice, who was severely infiltrated by the dark forces, had identified and worked to extricate herself from a number of destructive behavior patterns. One day during a therapy session, she looked at me wistfully. At the same time, there was a self-satisfied, smug smile on her lips. She announced, "I've just untangled my last pattern. I hope that my earthly mission will now be complete. I've been working so hard. I fantasized returning to the heavens, standing before God, and saying, 'This time I've finished, my Creator. Haven't I done well? Do with me what you will. I know I'll get the rewards I deserve.'"

I listened to Janice, astounded at the requests she—the cured one—was making of the Deity. I didn't intervene.

She continued, "My soul longed to hear from this Source, 'Welcome, my child. Well done.' I imagined myself bowing in humility, without a trace of narcissism, without the need to be considered special, without any vestige of possessiveness—without, without, without…Hadn't I worked on the *withouts* until I saw their kite tails wafting away into the ether, out of my psyche, out of my aura? To be free of them—no further scrutiny, no further effort, no more pain?"

She hesitated, expecting bravos for her poetic expression as well as her insights. When none was forthcoming and I simply continued to listen, Janice added, "Well, no sooner had I expressed these desires when I heard another voice roar at me, 'Of course. You're right. You should get rewards. Look at how hard you've been trying. See, nothing good happens without my intervention.' This voice justifies my asking for accolades and was most welcome to my now-victimized state because I was tired of trying and I wanted gratification for my efforts like—right now. What's wrong with that?"

"Janice, can you understand that this was a satanic voice? Responses like these come when lies and deceit are in operation," I explained, "when your motivation for doing things is askew and when you want special attention from God for your efforts. God rewards in his time and in his ways. If you project your un-giving parents onto him, you will remain in the patterns of behavior you've been trying to extricate yourself from since you were born."

Janice listened intently and said, "I understand what you're saying." She hesitated, and then went on to confess her next experience. "Fortunately, that voice was followed by an echo, becoming weaker and weaker until it was barely audible. It said, 'Who am I? Who? Huh?' I realized this was a remnant of my healthier self. But I also realized that some of those *withouts* were still around."

It was evident from her manner that Janice was pleased with herself and wanted me to believe that she had been redeemed. It was also clear that her need for rewards was still present. I thought, If only she were involved in her purging for the right reasons.

I explained, "Janice, these *withouts*, these patterns of behavior, do not lie idly in their nests, but are sniffed out by Satan's evil snoopers that act as standbys, eager to pounce upon your unfinished business. They're just waiting to brutalize an indulgent, lazy psyche with their merciless, torturous voices. Stay vigilant, conscious; desire above all to live by God's covenant. Don't worry about rewards. They'll be forthcoming when your heart wants to be in alliance only with the Deity."

"Does it ever end?" my patient wailed, slumping down in her seat. "Do I always have to be focused on righteousness, on change, on the ultimate pinnacle—a walk with God?"

"To that question my answer is an unequivocal yes!"

VICTIMIZATION

So often I have heard—and continue to hear—my patients and many other people make declarations such as, "But I had it so bad at home; how do you expect me to ever get over the pain of their abuse? Those wounds have scarred me for life!"

My response is, "How long do you want to take?" And my inference is, "How long do you want to coddle those wounds and pretend that they are your life?" When blame becomes the person's modus operandi, victimization is sure to follow.

Victimization keeps the person in a regressed position bordering on a *Not I* state. This state entices the ravenous nature of Satan through the person's laziness, indulgences, passive possessiveness, robotic mindlessness. The victim feels ever so sorry for himself or herself and therefore is wide open and receptive to what comes next—the vulturous satanic voices. Such people do not wish to live life as themselves. Little do they realize the nature of the guest they are inviting.

I recall trying to treat such a patient. In our first therapeutic session, I learned that she had had sixteen therapists before me. She related details of her abusive background with great relish. I felt as though I were on trial and that if I made any statement contradicting her assessment of herself, I would be convicted of treason.

Soon I became the seventeenth therapist who "didn't understand" her. She didn't truly want help. She wanted a sounding board for her travail—an expensive one, to say the least. It was predictable, too, that after two or three sessions she would introduce the plea of poverty. "My last therapist had a sliding scale; otherwise I can't afford to come."

The voice speaking to her, which I intuited, was saying, "You're important. Don't take her crap. You're smarter than this therapist is. She is learning from you. She's lucky to have you. Remember all the years you've spent in therapy."

After the third session, she canceled her next one properly and made no further appointments. She was listening to her voices, and since the City of New York is overflowing with psychotherapists, she will never be at a loss for setting her drama into action with yet another professional listener.

At that time, I was unskilled at recognizing and dealing with satanic infiltration, but I have learned much since then. This topic is a delicate one, and the right time to broach such a "whammy"—an expression coined by a patient who was slowly discovering her satanic voices—needs to be skillfully determined and handled.

It has also been my experience that when a person seeks therapeutic help but does not wish to look at himself or herself truthfully, that person will pounce on the concept of satanic infiltration when it is introduced and transfer their blame of the parents onto Satan. They will seize upon the newly introduced perpetrator of their pain like a desperate animal unexpectedly discovering a carcass and devouring it.

An individual who is unwilling to process and take responsibility for his or her own actions and choices will blame everything either on the parents or Satan—or both. The patient who wallows in victimization is acting like a willful, psychically arrested person, akin to a child. We are all susceptible to such limited thinking, which pervades the human race.

For example, I have been witness to people of faith who ignore the fact that their psyches are fallible; they blithely give their baggage to God and expect instant, miraculous intervention. They are not interested in working together with the Divine to come to a state of mature healing and integration. They do not admit their weakness or ask for God's help to heal. Instead, their victimized selves dump their load of unconsciousness on the Deity, feeling great relief, while they remain in the dark about the problems they have caused through their own choices.

This happens in many Christian churches where the Devil, "the Enemy," is seen as real and active in people's lives. Pastors and others who are responsible for the welfare of the flock often have no inkling—or ignore the fact—that Satan is not the only instigator of people's problems. But why would they? Does not Biblical Scripture tell humanity, "Honor your father and mother?" Why face the pain of processing parental abuse?

"That's a secular way of doing things," they say. New Age thinking and psychology are anathema to the Word and to the interpretation of the pastor and the church. And the very idea of a parental demonic voice would be considered a sin against the Holy Word. "Forgive them!" the pastor roars with divine conviction, with little understanding of what it takes to come to authentic healing.

"I'm trying," the believer tells himself or herself. "It's hard. I'm trying, but they molested me. I can't ignore this fact. My parents molested me! How do I forgive *that?*"

No one is available to tell the molested one to scream out indignation at the parental horror. This secret, confusing, festering reality remains stuck in the psyche and body of the abused. Do these preachings of the reverend take into consideration the woundedness of the one who has been so badly damaged? The ecclesiast, who most likely has never coped with his own woundedness, would be too overwhelmed by the reality of his parishioner's feelings to cope with that person's pain, much less be of help. In time, the voice of God inside the person dissipates, blurred by Satan's intermingled, contrapuntal cacophony: the voice of untruth, lies, deceit, intermixed with scriptural mouthing. Reality and truth become supplanted by dogma, and the psyche is left susceptible to the dark ones.

It has been my experience that most people need to work through their issues in a deliberate, step-by-step fashion. Victimized psyches need help to move forward to a more evolved state. The patient's psychic boundaries must be expanded to that of self-responsibility, which is vitally important for making sound choices in life. Self-responsibility will tax the will to its core, particularly in the face of satanic infiltration. But eventually, the psyche can arrive at divine wholeness.

But what if neither the therapist nor the pastor nor the patient has any inkling of satanic invasion, through the parents or by Satan itself? Then the patient will be unable to move out of his or her darkness and will remain fixated on the web of woe being spun. Possession, paranoia, and unreality—among other psychoses—are close by. It is important to remember that the dark forces love to infiltrate psyches that are riddled with dark thoughts and feelings: pain, guilt, hate, anger, willfulness, pride, envy, doubt, and alienation from the Source.

THE PARENTAL DEMONIC VOICE

> You're nothing, nobody
> Once a somebod; now a
> nobod □ a neutrisoma on
> a swing, a swing-swung
> organism going nowhere.
> Back and forth, that's all.
> You're nauseous, but
> expulsion from your mouth
> is stuck in your neutrisoma,
> And you feel safe, safe, safe,
> horribly safe. A neutrisoma
> in a straitjacket who declared
> bankruptcy a long time ago.

Such are the cacklings of sinister-ness by which we are affected—all of our lives. This is the voice of Satan, in its pure form. The parents become infiltrated and add their own sinister cacklings to that voice.

Under the influence of Satan, they address the desperate child in what I call the parental demonic voice:

> You little bastard. I'm going to get even
> for what you've done to me. If you had never
> been born, I would have been a great man. It's
> all your fault. Pay, prick. I want you to have
> a shitty life. I want you to feel bad, to loathe
> your body. You'll have no peace, never.
> You're my slave. Lose at everything.

This is the demonic voice of a patient's father who had become a puppet in the hands of Satan, a master puppeteer. There was no consciousness, no conscience, in the way he delivered his feelings to a desperate son. Destruction of the child was his only motivation. The father believed his litany. And the son was the victim to the demonic voice of the father, which is the voice of the infiltrated Satan, in the guise of the father's twisted, distorted, satanic perspective.

Man's inhumanity to man seems endless. What happened to that pure soul, formed and shaped by God's love? I have come to acknowledge that satanic forces are the wielders of such inhumanity—with the cooperation of man, himself, whether as a parent or as a lonely, bereft participant in life.

I describe the parental voices to be demonic because according to Webster's Dictionary, that which is demonic is evil, cruel, having a guiding spirit. The guiding spirit might be referred to as the Devil or Satan, the objectification of a hostile force external to our consciousness.

To firmly grasp what the parental demonic voice is, and where it comes from, we need to understand how a young child's inner development evolves. Put most simply, the voices stem from the superego, the groundbreaking concept given to us by Sigmund Freud. Freud claims that the superego came into being through introjections into the ego of the first objects of the id's libidinal impulses, namely the two parents. The superego retains the features of the introjected persons—their strengths, their weaknesses, their severity—and the child connects to the parents with an intensity that comes under the heading of *survival*. How?

As an example, the following is from a recorded hypnosis session in which a patient of mine named Kathe expressed her intense need to be fed by her mother—a mother who secretly but clearly never wanted her:

Come out of the cave and desperately need.
Can't see. Just smell and touch.
Put mouth to anything. Food. Air. Touch. Warmth.
Warmth. Food, breasts, teat, suck. Stay alive.
Keep heartbeat going. Suck hard. Regurgitate.
Breast bitter, milk sour.

So much space between me and her.
I reach. Feels like nails—claws.
I'm picked up so harshly.
Oops, up I go and down I
get thrown. Harsh! Why?
She doesn't want me!

Cold air. She's off again. I must get fed.
Why does she yell so? It pierces my flesh.
I feel frightened. Cold air between us.
I'll die from the draft.
She stays away longer and longer.
She might not return. Come back, horrible one.

I feel your brutality.
I need to have you as my mother to
fight my way out of the darkness
into the light. I've learned to hate—
hate
the
darkness.

I hate you, mother: evil, sick, devil.
But being with you is teaching me
how much I

want
the
light.

The war had begun, but that war had in fact already started in the womb, when the fetus was already experiencing that its environment would not be an accepting one.

The organism is hypersensitive to its environment both inside and outside the womb. It is well known that as early as six months, a fetus can sense the feelings and intentions of the mother. From that point on, it imbibes a constant flow of thoughts, feelings, and words from both parents.

At birth, the infant is a bundle of needs and desires. It is all mouth, hands, anal and urinary sphincters. Its needs must be met or it perishes. Its senses continue to intuit the feelings of the mother as well as other stimuli surrounding it. During this period in an infant's life, the senses of the organism are developing, and the brain matter is being impressed repeatedly by the world around it. These impressions are retained and lay the foundation for its perceptions about itself and its environment. Since these impressions are carved into a pure structure, it becomes difficult in later years to revise the effects of these impressions.

It is a time when the organism will either assert its God-given will and fight for its survival or submit to the will of the parent. For example, if the organism asserts its will and fights with a negative parent to retain its id impulses, a battle of wills follows that can be likened to the raging battle between two armies. Take the example of a parent who shouts to a whimpering or crying infant, "Don't cry or I'll give you something to cry about. I'll diaper you when I feel like it. You'll get fed in my time...If the parent's unconscious, demonic energy pervades, with its underlying demonic intention to destroy the organism's will or the organism itself, and projects unconsciously to the offspring, "I never wanted you...I wish you were dead, you filthy, smelly kid," then the organism will quickly squelch itself from acting on its *id* impulses rather than die. Floundering, weak, vulnerable, and desperate, it becomes a perfect victim for the dark ones.

The parent's denial of the child's needs is a powerful energy. The child becomes fixated by that "no" stance of the parent, the way the cobra dances to the tune of its jail keeper's instrument. Breathlessly the child waits for that rare time when the "no" becomes a "yes." The organism then feels *validated*. Otherwise it does not exist. Nonexistence bred from lack of validation creates a susceptibility to the dark forces. *Seeking and acquiring validation* becomes the child's *modus operandi*: What was it I did right? I'll remember and do that the next time to get Mommy's or Daddy's smile and acceptance. In this way, the organism begins its journey into the *Not I* state and infiltration by the evil energy.

To compensate for its feeling of nonexistence, the organism begins to emulate the parent to experience those moments of validation. It begins to incorporate the negative energy as an all-powerful image. The child's needs go underground, so to speak, with a silent vow: "When I grow up, I'll be as powerful as you are and get whatever I want." In the meantime, its godly, truthful self is submerged as he watches in awe and in fear the parental figure strut before him, all knowing, all powerful, all everything.

The organism's own needs, birthed from its divine core, hide away, saluting, bowing, scraping, and smiling, as servant to the master. The self has found a way to stay safe; and in some cases, just barely alive. The *id* needs are suppressed and the ego is splintered. What becomes dominant are the shoulds and should nots of the parent's superego and the underlying intentions that create the parental demonic voices. This energy becomes the organism's identity. *The voices are born.*

Because of the organism's repressed needs that make it vulnerable to the unconscious intention of the parental figures, the child's *aura* (which I discuss in the next section) becomes susceptible to penetration by that intention. And the child's *reactions* to the negative *intention* of the parent become his *ego*, in which he is trapped and possessed.

It is in this egoical form that the organism functions. Attracted to this demonic energy, the child also incorporates into his or her bodily structure the structure of the parent from whom these messages are derived. The organism becomes encased, not only psychically, but physically—becoming *the embodiment of the parental superego and its underlying demonic intention*. The result is relative and ranges from sanity to insanity.

All of humankind is subjected to this phenomenon. An illustration by a Christian author writing in the fifth century C.E., Cyril of Jerusalem, makes this phenomenon even clearer:

> ...the unclean devil, when he comes
> upon the soul of a man...comes like
> a wolf upon a sheep, ravening for blood
> and ready to devour. His presence is
> most cruel; the sense of it most oppressive;
> the mind is darkened; his attack is an
> injustice also, and the usurpation of another's
> possession. For he tyrannically uses another's
> body, another's instruments, as his own
> property; he throws down him who stands
> upright; he perverts the tongue and distorts
> the lips. Foam comes instead of words; the
> man is filled with darkness; his eye is
> open, yet his soul sees not through it.[8]

THE HUMAN AURA OR ENERGY FIELD

I have talked about the voices, the superego, the intention of the parental superego—all part of the demonic onslaught—but there is another energetic component that explains why the organism is an open channel for the parents' negative penetration into the organism's vulnerable psyche: the human aura. John Pierrakos, a former Bioenergetic psychiatrist, was gifted in seeing the human aura or energy field. He explained the phenomenon in this way:

> All living organisms are surrounded by a
> radiating luminous envelope which
> pulsates at a specific rate and has specific
> layering, hue and structure. This envelope
> cast of another body of energy which
> penetrates the physical body and spreads
> its luminous radiation outwards in the
> periphery and is perceived as the energy
> field or aura of that organism...it is very
> sensitive and responds to emotional and

79

physical states and has specific characteristics
in illness and health.[9]

He further explains how the energy field can create the warping and distortion of the child's ego:

> People affect each other's energy field
> since the field constantly surrounds us and
> contacts the field of the neighboring person
> or groups of people. We are living in each
> other's field when we are in close proximity.
> The physical body mirrors what is happening
> in the energy field. The physical body seems
> to reflect the state of the energy field which
> shows many times pathological changes which
> become structural at a later date in the organs
> and tissues.[10]

The energy field or aura links us to one another with invisible strands of energy through which we interact, for the most part unconsciously. Words are less consequential than the energy vibration contained in the unconscious exchange of thoughts and feelings between people. This interpenetration of the child's aura with the parents' auras forges a bond between them, making separation almost impossible.

Both Wilhelm Reich and Alexander Lowen advocated self-regulation as a healthy way to rear a child, because they were aware of the innate wisdom the organism has about its own needs. They have both stated that after birth, too much outer stimulation will interfere with the infant's ability to stay contained within its own structure. Here they are referring to intrusion into the child's aura by the auras of visiting relatives, friends, and neighbors who are present to sing their praises to the new arrival and to parenthood.

The newborn struggles with great intensity not only to be in a physical body but to adjust to this world and, in doing so, cannot manage the amount of outer stimulation the parents often foist upon it. Nor is sibling rivalry an idle concept. Any other unnecessary stimulation from others' confused psyches—not to mention auras filled with negation—

will be detrimental to a newborn whose susceptibility to the demonic is a serious matter indeed.

As a young child's ego develops, it is especially difficult for a healthy connection to occur between parent and child when the bond that has been woven is constructed of negative, demonic fabric. Why are we especially susceptible to onslaught by a perverted parental mind? Why do we become infatuated and incorporate the energy of the parent who is the more oppressive to us? Why do we not concentrate on the parent who is more emotionally available? Negation has an indescribable power for most people, outweighing feelings of love. This is because we are all products of generationally, satanically infiltrated parents. Our hearts have frozen; our minds have stagnated from untruths; and we have become ripe, juicy morsels for the evil forces. Pierrakos describes this power:

> ...the very tensions of the character attitudes
> of negation generate excitement. Forces are
> pressing on the person, conflicting forces that
> take him in their grip; the movement of energy
> versus the countermovement of blockage. I
> have looked at the aura of people when they are
> actively engaged in denial, and I can assure you
> that the more they go from neutrality to negation,
> the more their energy field brightens, and the
> faster it pulsates. Thus there is energetic
> excitement in negation. This excitement is
> often misunderstood as a free flow of energy,
> and is chosen by the person as an alternative
> to an absence of feeling—a deadness.[11]

Demonically oriented parents—those who have an absence of self but who become alive in a state of negation—fit Pierrakos's description of psychic deadness. His explanation clarifies how the child's loss of power under the domination of a warped, negative parent makes the child susceptible to such energy. The youngster perceives the parent as omnipotent and omniscient, a powerful giant. And the child finds this manifestation desirable because it wishes to reclaim its own power through the parent's example.

Deadness is frightening because it promises a lack of feeling, and that lack can be dangerous. Has it not been reported repeatedly that neighbors who witnessed a horrendous crime have told newspaper reporters, "I don't understand—he was such a well-behaved person, a churchgoer, too." Such deadness of self can be likened to the bizarre example of Adolph Hitler, who, in the 1930s and 1940s, bellowed forth to massive German audiences his negative tirades about the Jews, the Poles, the gypsies—all those who were not Aryans. His ranting took the German people's focus off their impoverished postwar state, their economic destitution, and hopelessness.

The magnetic charge or negation—the "glamour" of it—often substitutes for, although it doesn't satisfy, the emotional nourishment the child craves. Mistaking the negativity as intimate contact, the child is diverted from focusing on its intuitive sense that it is not really wanted and loved. These are devastating realizations that will make the young one turn to Satan or other self-destructive means to try and protect itself.

The reality of negation's devastating effect was observed by Dr. Pierrakos, whose patient sat next to a plant for one hour during a session. Pierrakos reports:

> I had a flowering white chrysanthemum plant on my office desk when one of my patients entered complaining and whining about her depressed state. She sat next to the plant. It had had a field…of an inner light blue color of beautiful brilliance with gold streams in the outer field, pulsating 14 to 16 times a minute. In a short time as she spoke, the pulsations almost vanished to 2 to 3 times a minute. The brilliance of the field disappeared and there was a slight gray emanation during its pulsation.[12]

I inherited this patient a year later. I can recall that after each session I began to feel like the chrysanthemum: drained and pale, with a yellowish color replacing my usual rosy complexion. I began to dread the sessions with her; but at the same time, I was fascinated by the amount of incessant negativity coming from this diminutive person. I was waiting, like a child, for the negativity to cease so that my psyche could relax and my body could release itself from its rigid defensiveness.

I also was mesmerized, eagerly anticipating a glimmer of light, of hope, of joy. It never happened. I recall that after she left the sessions, I would run to open the windows for fresh air; I would blow out from my mouth and nostrils the contaminated air I had ingested from the patient. I wanted to purge myself from her dark energy by drenching my body under a cold shower. Such is the reaction of a conscious adult. We can now wonder how an onslaught of this nature would affect a young, sensitive organism with little consciousness. We might wonder, too, whether such is the time when the organism silently, unconsciously calls out for help while the dark forces are standing by ready to invade the caller.

THOSE WHO CALL

When I asked my patients to recall their first experience of the evil forces penetrating them, one woman responded, "At the moment I was born. My soul knew this would be a loveless life and so I allowed the dark forces to attach themselves to me. Was I conscious of what I was doing? Of course not. I was just born, but my soul knew. Could she stop me? No! I was too unconscious and I needed comfort—that's all I was capable of sensing. Comfort! Comfort! Comfort!"

A male patient offered, "I was hungry and cried a lot. Then my father threw me against the wall like a doll. I landed in the crib—fortunate for me, or maybe not. I didn't cry, but I lay still and just looked at him. I don't remember clearly, but at that moment it seemed as though something dark slipped into my body and I felt more powerful."

The third response was, "I was two years old. It was clear to me that my mother didn't want me. Couldn't I figure out what that meant at the time? I could not; but I knew I needed help from somewhere."

I asked the patient who had been thrown against the wall as an infant—a tactic used by the Nazis in concentration camps to destroy the newly born—how he remembered the incident. He replied, "I don't remember, because I was too little, but my parents told me this story when I was older. They laughed about it…found it hilarious!"

They laughed about it…found it hilarious! What better example can be given of a situation where the parent is in a state of negation and is dead—not dead, but imprisoned by the dark forces? The child observes the parental reaction and becomes invalidated. He or she thinks there must be something wrong with me because I don't think it's funny. The ha-ha-ha's continue to reverberate in the child's psyche along with 'There's something wrong with me.'

In the next chapter, we will penetrate more deeply into just how the parental demonic voices such as these do their work of destruction in the human being.

CHAPTER 2
EXPOSING THE PARENTAL DEMONIC VOICES

I, too, was a victim of the parental demonic voices; I first discovered this during the years when I was a professional dancer. The moment I stepped onstage, began to speak in public, or to audition—events that required a supernormal unity of body, mind, and spirit—a disastrous split would occur in this unity. A voice began to bellow into my whole being, "You're not good enough! Who do you think you are? You're ugly. Who would want to look at you? Ha-ha! You almost tripped. You're not a dancer!"

The voices roared as my body glided through the movements I'd rehearsed for many weeks. I fought against those voices by ignoring them, but the more I ignored them, the louder and more insidious they became. In one performance, when the dance ended I ran to the dressing room in tears. "Nobody likes me," I sobbed.

"Are you crazy?" the stagehand commented. "Listen to the applause. Take another curtain call."

"No!" I shrieked. "Nobody likes me. I'm not a dancer." I had succumbed to the evil voices and was carrying around with me a shadow, another self, a doppelganger:

> They're voices in my head.
> They rattle on like sputtering geese.
> Do this, do that, my way, not yours.
> Cry out, cry out, but not too loud.

Restraint, restraint is so important.
Go all the way, but maybe not.
You're tired, aren't you?
Go to sleep—but if you sleep,
you'll miss the action.
Confusing, isn't it?
Be simple, child. Give up.
Just listen to your doppelganger,
that bears no malice for anyone.

Mamma had said to her daughter, "You want to dance? You?" The question was a simple one, indeed, but loaded with an underlying intention, and I, a sensitive, tender, deer-like organism, felt mutilated, ravaged, torn apart by her underlying proclamation.

It was demonic. What I heard was, "You're not good enough. Who do you think you are? You'll fall, for sure. You can't have what I didn't have."

My ego reflected her simple statement. Her prophecy taunted me until, from its unbearable weight, I could neither fully breathe nor stand up straight. Stuck inside her prophetic rubble, it was as though I were choking and groaning to my ruthless monarch:

Your voices reek
of slime and malice.
I'll fight you hard
until they're vanquished.
If not,
I'd rather die.

I fight you like a Don Quixote—
sightless, wild, terrified.
I lance you, lance you
with my paper spear.
It makes you laugh uproariously.
I freeze, immobilized.
I sink into oblivion, but
pray and hope for a miraculous rescue—

by a friend, an ally, even…
God! Where are you, God?
Do you remember me?
Do you remember? Do you?
He's not around!
Simply not on my frequency.

I'm not a dancer," the voices
continue. "Don't watch
me. Watch the others only.
I'm a failure, a nobod. She
must be right. Aren't
mothers their daughters'
oracles?

When I think of the years of anguish these voices caused me, as well as the anguish the people in my practice endured because of their own demonic voices, I could kick myself to the periphery of the planet for my unbelief, which kept me from pursuing this topic from my own perspective. Psychotherapists initially encourage their patients to blame their abusive parents for the suffering that was caused, as well they should. Since this truth is only the tip of the iceberg, however, it is my contention that patients need to probe further. In doing so, they would realize that Satan is controlling the parental psyche. Unwillingness to question such areas of conflict or to use methods beyond standard therapeutic procedures sets the psychotherapist and the patient on a fast-moving merry-go-round from which they never get off and from which the patient is eventually reduced to a Not I state.

ENCOUNTERING DEMONIC RAGE

The manifestations of people's reactions to the parental demonic voices differ widely from person to person. I am sometimes struck by the demonic look in the eyes behind the eyes. We are all masked to be accepted in society, and thus our persona achieves a presence in full, false regalia. When, during therapy, this mask is challenged, the terror, the despair, and the demonic rage are visible.

The evil that has been hidden beneath a thin layer of civility is called forth in all its fury as soon as a patient is given the opportunity to express himself or herself. When I worked in this way with a patient named Bruce, his voice changed to a choking hoarseness; his eyes bulged and his jaw protruded; his fists clenched until the knuckles became white. Bruce's body assumed the stance of something grotesque and evil.

"I'll kill you," he screamed as he hit the bed. "Don't ask for one more thing, or it'll be the end of you."

"Who is that?" I asked.

"My father."

"He lives inside you," I commented.

"Big time," Bruce responded. "What's he doing inside me—so vivid, so clear—when all I want to do is hide from him and am terrified of him?"

"You've imbibed him," I explained.

"Why would I want to imbibe someone so evil?"

"Because his dark negative energy appeals to you. It feels powerful and invincible, and unconsciously you want to emulate him. In emulating him, you absorb his evil, an evil that is generational.

"Right now you feel like a victim, but in time you'll discover your own dormant rage rising against his demonized brutality. This rage lies like a sleeping beast not too far beneath the surface. If you choose to stay passive, you'll fall into despair and pay homage to victimization all of your life. As a perpetual victim, you attract more brutality; and worst of all, your true self atrophies and becomes attacked, not only by other humans, but most importantly, by other hellish spirits."

"I don't want that!"

"Then fight, Bruce. Have the courage to battle the evil in your nature. Bring light to your consciousness. Live with God on your side."

When the voices have been detected and diligently worked on, they disappear. The person is left with an I, because the diminishing or vanquishing of the parental demonic voices promotes an I in the psyche of the person, whose life can then be reclaimed. Adversities, pain, struggle—sometimes disgust and impatience with one's repetitive choices that stagnate living and life, engendering familiar misdeeds—can cause the self to scream out to the universe for help. Glimmers of light might then rekindle the person's desire for a larger horizon from which to live and listen to the voice of God.

Each soul has her own destiny, her own appetite, and her own time frame for salvation. Often, when a person has worked for a long time on these issues, the desire to be finished, complete, whole can generate impatience and sometimes a deep resistance—or even an unwillingness—to keep going.

THERE IS MORE…

I once conducted a workshop whose participants had worked diligently on their psyches for many years. At one point, I said to them, "There is more, there is more…" and immediately the room fell into silence. The atmosphere had been charged with excited, bustling energy; now I could feel an almost ominous resistance in the space. I was mystified. "What's up?" I asked. "Aren't you excited to evolve further?"

Gloria, a valorous soul, took the initiative and spoke up. "Does it ever end?"

"Does what ever end?" I asked, interested in her frustration.

"Well, since we've eradicated the parental demonic voices, I hoped that would be the end of probing. Now you're saying we have to deal with the satanic voices as well. I feel that I'm living life as though every tentacle, every nerve, every molecule, every atom has to be constantly poised and focused so that I become who I really am. And now you tell us that there's more!"

I realized that I had asked myself the same questions not too long before and had made the same weary comments to myself. I shared my reactions with the group, as well as my conviction that the desire to grow varies from individual to individual. I told them that it was my desire to be as squeaky clean as I could be when I meet my Maker and that this desire has been present since I was eleven years old. I recalled my eleven-year-old consciousness, which told me, if you shirk your karma now, you'll have to return to finish it at another time in another life. So do it now!

My eleven-year-old self couldn't spell the words karma and reincarnation or know their meaning. Was it God's voice speaking to me? I would say yes to that question. This voice pushed me into life to find what I've been discovering ever since. Am I glad? Very glad. Has it been a difficult journey? Very, very difficult. Yet I do not regret God's whisperings.

Did the promptings of the eleven-year-old continue? Most likely, but I didn't hear them. If I did, I cast them aside to continue with my Not I existence. The pain and distortions I lived from became predictable and were defined as living. I continued to listen not only to the parental demonic voices but to the satanic as well.

After I explained all of that to the group, I added, "But in the past few years, God's promptings have become more audible to me; I now listen to these promptings avidly because I want God in my life. This might not be everyone's desire, but it is mine. The choice is yours."

"Let's meditate on what we want," Gloria chimed in, once again her exuberant self. Her suggestion broke the silence for the other members as they took seats on their back jacks, closed their eyes, and placed their upright palms on their thighs. The room became filled with the sweet ease of loving, expectant natures. Soon, everyone in the group huddled together. Gloria, the spokeswoman, announced the verdict. God's wisdom had spoken, "It will end. Soon. Do your probing ceaselessly, with conviction and truth. Listen to my voice only. Satan's voice will then atrophy."

With that counsel, I read to them a quote about Satan from Scott Peck's last book, Glimpses of the Devil:

> The devil…is a spirit that is powerful.
> It may be in many places at the same time
> and manifest itself in a variety of distinctly
> paranormal ways. It is thoroughly malevolent.
> Its only motivation seems to be the destruction
> of human beings or the entire human race. It
> is deceitful, vain, capable of taking up a kind
> of residence within the mind, brain, soul or
> body of willing human beings.[13]

As we continued, I explained that the first step is to recognize the voice of Satan, which is a more conscious and deliberate voice than the parental demonic voice. The satanic voice is more insidious, mesmerizing the psyche with its persuasive, soothing, confident, and seemingly caring qualities. I told them that I, too, had been mesmerized at the beginning of my satanic exploration. I gave an example of its soothing manner whenever I would try to write.

> You want to write? Good! But, not today.
> Let me guide you. But not today—tomorrow.
> Begin the next day. You need sleep.
> Lots of it. No, you're not lazy. Just sleepy.
> We all need sleep. It takes a lot of energy
> to write. Let me help you. Don't worry.
> Tomorrow, you'll be clearer.
> Listen to me, no one else. Sleep. That's good.
> But tomorrow…

"Awesome!" exclaimed one of the members. "It's really soothing, almost irresistible."

"You're right," I told her. "If you're susceptible to its power, which prevents you from doing anything without its input, you can't create anything worthwhile on your own. The days turn into weeks, months, and years, and—as I have witnessed from others' attempts to create— the creation never happens.

As you can see, Satan's voice, although more deliberate, is more subtle, and less "in your face," so to speak, than the parental demonic voice. Satan's agenda is to entice the human being with cunning and deceit to bring him to Sheol or hell. By contrast, the parent vents its ugly feelings unrestrainedly, out of control, unconsciously, because the underbelly of such feelings is generationally induced. So the more aware we can be of what the voices sound like, the better equipped we are for the battle against them.

CHAPTER 3
RECOGNIZING THE SATANIC VOICES

"What do the voices sound like?" I asked the members of the workshop, who had limited experience with these voices. At first, they were baffled. But after a long pause, one person said, "They're like a vibration, a ringing in the ears, a buzzing from far away. It's not really a voice."

"Is it like communicating with another's energy field?" I asked, helping them with a concept they had probed at a previous time.

"Yeah," said a member, a big grin creasing her face. "Yeah, it's really not a voice, but a thought—a thought in the form of a vibration that has no form or shape—like a cloud that forms, changes its form, then disappears. It's kind of vaporous, but it leaves an imprint on your psyche. I feel it, hear it, see it enough to draw it. Weird."

"That's a good description," I told her.

"It's similar to the parental demonic voices," said another participant. "Except those voices are more tangible. Maybe it's because the demonic intention is hidden underneath what the parents are saying, which makes the meaning of what is being said to the child clearer and more immediate. The impact is stronger, therefore, when you get slaughtered by their demonic intention."

I nodded at her astuteness. They were excited and their imaginations were flowing.

"The satanic voices seem to be light-years away by comparison to the parental demonic voices when they attack," added Victoria. "Maybe it's because Satan is capable of pretending to be God—soft-spoken, kind, caring."

"Maybe," I ventured.

"That could be the reason why I sometimes don't know whose voice I'm listening to: Satan's or God's. And why I have to carefully figure out what the message is telling me instead of accepting it verbatim."

I nodded in agreement.

"What a world!" she continued. "I've finally recognized the voices, and now I have to decipher whose they are, or I'll get lost again. Don't God's voice and the angels' voices seem light-years away, too, the same as with the satanic voices?"

"It would seem so," was my response. "But clear attunement to God's voice through fervent prayer will enable you to contact him and to hear his counsel. In this way, you will gain the right perception of whose voice is contacting you. It's also true that most of us who are searching for a real self are adamant about rejecting Satan's voice in our psyches."

I waited a while, and then repeated my last statement. When no one responded, I realized I needed to be more forthright. "One of you is unwilling to relinquish your connection to Satan. I surmise that its voice seems all-powerful to you and gives you the semblance of security." Having said this, I turned to the person I was referring to. "I've heard you quote from this voice, Harriet, which tells you:

> Stay with me.
> I'm your everything.
> I'm your companion,
> your mate.
> I'll satisfy all of your
> empty places.
> I'm everything you need."

"Yup, that's the voice I hear," said Harriet, relieved to make her confession. "It makes me feel good. I'm not sure I want to give it up," she admitted. "It's been with me since I was born. I know for a fact that my mother didn't want me, and here's something or someone who does. You'll have to convince me that I'm mistaken."

"I understand your reluctance and your temptation, Harriet. It's a persuasive voice giving you the security that a parent should have given from the beginning of your life. I wonder if you understand that unless you extricate yourself from this evil predator, your soul—the essence of God's substance—will become weakened and erode. A state of worthlessness will supplant your once stalwart vigor. Soon you will no longer feel worthy to hear God's voice, and Satan's falsities will intensify. Your connection to God will diminish, and the repetitive circle of worthlessness in its many variations will take over. You will complain about God's abandonment. It is you, however, who will have abandoned him. God never abandons us.

"But because your psyche has been warped by the evil voices, you have become blocked, too blocked to hear clearly if at all. When one is split in one's allegiance to the Creator and Satan, that person is in a serious struggle—not unlike the strife that was in Lucifer at the beginning of time. Are not you and all of us in the same conflict as Adam and Eve were as told in Genesis of the Old Testament? How long will it take for us to learn which one to follow? Perhaps now is our time to make that choice. I hope so."

By now, everyone in the group had gathered around Harriet. Her tears were flowing, her chest heaving from the pain of her aloneness. The others cradled her and rocked her with nurturance she had never received as a child. Her sobs continued; and the more she sobbed, the better she felt. What I continued to tell them was meant not only for Harriet but for all of us who had suffered from the parental emotional abuse that had made us so susceptible to the evil influences.

"Your parents didn't, couldn't, wouldn't love you, Harriet. Any or all of these might be true. Experience the pain of it, the loss, the loneliness such a state causes. Doing this, you will feel anguishing pain, but the tears you shed will wash the pain away and bring a more real and stronger connection to your self. Can you agree with this fact, Harriet?"

"It's like a baptism," she told us, sobbing and laughing at the same time.

"Know also that one's persistence to behave from a deprived, victimized pattern such as: I had it so bad; nobody's suffering is worse than mine. Poor me, I can't do it for myself, leads to untold disappointment. The tendency of a person searching to make up for the absence of a mother's or father's love is to turn people into idols who will become deified substitute parents. When these idols do not fulfill our expectations, however, all involved in this drama will become enraged: The victim, because he or she is painfully disappointed that the symbiotic behavior aborts; the idols, because they sense how the victim is using them fraudulently to steer the victim out of their Not I-ness without mobilizing their own efforts. The result is that the victim unwittingly invites Satan's uncanny, standby shrewdness into the psyche. And in this way, Satan will keep a person fixated on such a pattern, making the victim its companion and mate to finally usurp the soul."

Harriet walked over to where I was standing. Her face looked cleansed; her gratitude was overwhelming. She hugged me with the strength of a bear, and then she went to her seat and held hands with those who had taken their seats on either side of her. I heard her say to me telepathically, "You said there would be more. Okay, I'm ready for more."

I smiled at her with heartfelt warmth and answered not only her but also the other members:

"Whatever voice you invite into your psyche is your choice. If you invite God's voice while your feelings and thoughts are swimming in negativities you will have to understand that the energy field surrounding your head and the rest of your body will broadcast that. It is a known fact that the light coming from your aura will then have breaks in its pulsations. These breaks and gaps prevent the heavenly world from receiving your call and contacting you. It is as though the transmission between you and the heavenly world had static, and neither of you hears the other.

"Is this not why Jesus fasted for forty days and forty nights in the wilderness to cleanse his entire being—to make himself a perfect receptacle for the voice of his Father?

"When negativities are a part of your nature, Satan and its cohorts feed upon them, and these evil forces begin to occupy your head—encompassing the third eye or optic thalamus, the center known to have supernormal vision. When that chakra or energy center is blocked, the organs in proximity to this chakra—the eyes, ears, nose, mouth, and throat—are also in darkness. The rest of the body follows. The being is then imprisoned by the evil forces. In such darkness, the soul pivots around its own axis, desperately searching for a direction.

"The road to God is blocked by one's own doing, from having wallowed in a victimized state. Darkness, loss of self, death, even hell becomes a preferable choice for the person.

"Once in hell, the person's agony is indescribable, as has been written about by Emanuel Swedenborg, an eighteenth-century philosopher, scientist, and theologian, who was given the divine gift of literally contacting heaven and hell. According to him, hell is a state and a place where every soul is hopelessly lost to itself, the way it was during the soul's existence on Earth, but worse. Any reference to the higher realm is anathema to Satan and the other spirits in hell; and the one making the reference is categorically punished. Incarceration is complete.

"But, remember, we do have choices. Yes, it is true that we come into this incarnation with baggage, baggage that forces us to do our earthly homework. But if we are diligent and grateful for the opportunity, life becomes a taskmaster through which we learn, evolve, and progress. Let me be fanciful and quote from an enlightened person's conversation with God on the topic of free will. She is endowed with the ability to channel God's wisdom. The following excerpt is the information she was given:

> *I, God, want conscious angels in my realm*
> *with individualized wisdom, able to adapt*
> *themselves to higher frequencies of*
> *understanding. Humanity, in general, is lazy,*
> *no match for the cunning Lucifer, whose evil*
> *and never-changing rage at me will continue*
> *to enslave my creation.*
>
> *Whom do you choose? Do you want*
> *my heaven or its hell? Choose well,*
> *my beloveds. I say mine, not Satan's.*
> *It creates nothing but malice. I realize that*
> *in times of deep anguish, the soul resorts*
> *to vengeance to ward off malice. She need*
> *know, however, that in turning to me, anguish*
> *will be supplanted by wisdom, love, truth.*
> *Redemption will be swift; salvation immediate;*

resurrection-transformation my lover's gift
to you.

Wake up! Do not continue to be burned by
Hell's fires until the soul is charred to a
flaky crisp—often her demise. Do not make
me weep and weep as do the angels at
humanity's soul delusions,
its lazy grip on itself, its fatuous involvement
with my lost Lucifer.

Humanity, hear my plea. I need your love.
I starve from your crumbs. My pain to see
you walk willingly into my opponent's
abyss, your unwillingness to call my name,
to see your heedless, reckless soul abortions
grieves me, as a loving parent would be grieved
at your desecration.

Tell this to all who have ears to hear.
The free will I give will hopefully not have to
prevail for much longer—for other eternities.
Instead, let my sheep know their shepherd and run
home willingly.

"The message is clear. The choice is ours. 'You have only yourself to blame' is the cliché many offspring hear from their parents. We step into the darkness, not knowing what to do. We emerge, we act, and the choice has been made. We become more defined, more of self. Do we ever contemplate at such a crucial moment whether our souls have chosen God or the evil one? Time will tell. If only God would tweak our noses, our chins, or ears to monitor our choices. It's up to us to ask for his intervention. Why didn't I think of doing that? we wonder, slapping ourselves lightly on the forehead. Blame ensues: SATAN? You MONSTER! We become aware of our reprimand to Satan that is followed by more consciousness: Am I looking for justification by blaming all on it? No, it's not Satan. It's me! Reason tells me that. Free will, I hate you because your ramifications do not lie.

"However"—I paused dramatically, undecided, but determined at the same time. "There is another step we have to take to get out of the grip of Satan."

"Nooooo!" they yelled in unison.

We all laughed at the spontaneity of their unexpected uproar. "You do want to get out of Satan's grip, don't you?" I asked.

"What do we have to do?" called out Harriet, at the frontline of such a desire.

"You've got to forgive the abusers." The words came out as though I had just asked them whether they would like another cup of tea.

"What!" screamed Harriet. "You must be kidding! Forgive my hateful parents?"

"Forgive the father who molested me?" screamed another member, on the verge of apoplexy.

"A mother who beat me for no reason, threw me against a hot steam pipe that could have maimed me for life? Are you crazy, Dr. Anneliese?"

"Forgive a mother who ignored me her entire life because I was the third son and wasn't born a girl?" spat out a man in the group, red from indignation. "She made me her surrogate lover because my dad, the gynecologist, was too busy taking care of his patients' vaginas, professionally and personally. Do you have any idea how this lover relationship with my mom stunted me as a man? To this day I can't make a normal commitment to a woman for fear she'll enslave me forever. And you want me to forgive this bitch of a mother?"

"Whoa! Whoa!" I shouted, outstretching my two arms to calm them down. "I understand your outbursts—believe me I do. I was in the same boat as you are. I admit that in the face of your pain and fury, forgiving seems almost impossible to do, but this doesn't mean you shouldn't strive to do it. We all have goals. Some aspects of our goals can be mastered more easily than others; others take more time before they can be understood and given their rightful attention. Approach forgiveness in that way, and before you are aware, forgiving will no longer seem like you're capitulating to the abusers. Instead, you will see that the abusers have given you a rare opportunity to expand your nature, a nature that will experience the high frequency of God's nature.

"Without forgiving, you lose the ability to be allied with God. You will stay stuck in your past, focused on its unfairness, on your feelings of vindictiveness, rage, desperation, lostness, hate—your victimization. These feelings, as I have said repeatedly, lend themselves to continuous ensnarement by the evil forces. Forgiving will free you of such incarceration and open the horizon to your connection to God, to a larger Self, your I Am. God will respond to such a being, and the past will recede. A new person will evolve—reconstructed, whole, united to the creation you intrinsically are. I know that innately you all want this."

They became quiet, spontaneously reseating themselves in their back jacks with their eyes closed. I held my breath, anticipating more opposition, until several minutes later I heard a raspy whisper coming from Harriet, who seemed to be praying out loud:

> God, I don't want to stay stuck with Satan
> as my guide. I confess that I don't want it.
> I want your counsel. If it means forgiving
> my horrible parents, I'll forgive them. I don't
> feel it from my heart, yet; but maybe in time, I
> will. Please help me do this. Amen.

Like a chorus, the rest of the members said, "Amen." They were clearly in accord with her plea. They remained seated, their psyches apparently in surrender to an I Am state. Their meditative smiles revealed glimmers of transformation as the workshop drew to a close. While I bathed in their tranquility, I thought to myself that our own psychological Not I state can be likened to living in hell. Every prisoner dominated by the darkness but with a modicum of self schemes to find a way out of incarceration.

I have discovered that living on this planet is an ever-probing, restless search for the self. Looking for the self is an eternal mystery orchestrated by God and his angels, who are relentless in their desire to have the souls of each human being achieve wholeness. The next mystery is then sensitively devised by the celestials so that overwhelm can be subtly but adventurously handled by our psyches until the threshold to our unraveling has been crossed and we are on another path—the path to another piece of the puzzle of who we truly are.

I say in my first book: *My Female, My Male, My Self and God: A Modern Woman in Search of Her Soul*: "There is more, there is more, that much I know. Lead the way. I will follow."[14]

I have found a way to free the soul by a construct, a method to unlock the prisoner's cell door. This method identifies the parental demonic voices as well as the generationally hidden satanic voices encased in the parents' intention. I, personally, have benefited from its use as have the people I teach. In the next chapter, I present it to the reader.

Chapter 4
The Construct for Processing the Parental Demonic Voices

The relationship between psychological and spiritual healing is deep and complex, and the core of my work for the past twenty years has been to unravel some of the mysteries of that relationship. The Parental Demonic Construct works successfully in both these realms, initiating healing and the reclaiming of the self. How and why does this happen?

When a person working within the construct is able to express himself or herself in a way that was not possible as a child because the parental demonic voices created havoc in its psyche, that person will again have access to a real self. In reclaiming the nature and energy of a renewed self, the person can come forward into life and live with conviction and strength. This is what I mean when I say that a person changes from the Not I state to becoming predominantly an I.

In devising the parental demonic construct, I needed to see the beliefs that were at the root of the Not I state. I noticed that my patients were riddled with an "I can't" mentality, and this gave me the clue that the voices in the psyche were active and dominant, preventing the person from being in charge of himself or herself. It's as though the psyche were enveloped in gauze, a veil that created a split between consciousness and semi-consciousness—and sometimes, depending upon the thickness of the gauze, unconsciousness. It seemed as though the being were dominated by unseen forces, like a puppet handled by an invisible puppeteer.

When I asked the patient, "Why do you feel incapable of doing such and such?" the answer invariably was, "I don't know. I just can't." I realized that the demonic energy had gripped the soul of the person and was flailing it around like a wild animal with a captured trophy. Hoping to unmask the demonic voices, I proceeded to break down the "I can't" belief with the following process:

1. I ask the patient to vocalize and physicalize this "I can't" belief. The person is directed to walk and talk from this "I can't" energy. As this energy is being vocalized and physicalized, the expressive feelings that come from him might be: "I feel like a piece of shit' or "I'm so stupid' or "I feel so worthless.'

2. I ask the patient to exaggerate the voices and intensify the body gestalt or configuration. For example, the feet might be ungrounded, the pelvis tucked under, the chest collapsed, the mouth in a grimace, and the breathing constricted. When a specific physical pattern with its accompanying voice is simulated, the patient will recognize it as the gestalt of one of its parents.

3. I ask the patient to imagine a circle with the identified parent standing at the head of the circle. (Illustration 1) The patient sits in the center of the circle, facing the parent.

4. I ask the patient to remember something specific told to him in the past by one of his parents and to speak that out loud. (Illustration 2) For example, "The guests are coming any minute. Comb your hair. Make yourself presentable." Since the parent's statements—as well as the tone of voice and other cues besides the words themselves—convey an energetic component that projects itself from the parent's aura to the child's, the child senses this energy and reacts to it. The parent, either consciously or unconsciously, has an underlying intention. In this case, the intention is anything but supportive or even neutral. This negative, harmful intention is what I refer to as the demonic voice. In Illustration 2, the demonic voice is speaking to the child. The child's interpretation of this voice will be something like this: "You're a nuisance. Why don't you know what to do? Are you stupid?"

5. The patient, as his or her child-self, reacts to the demonic voice. (Illustration 3) The reaction to the demonic voice becomes internalized, establishing the ego from which the child functions. In reacting to the demonic voice, the child's egoic voice might say, "I feel so useless, so unclear, and stupid. Why can't I do anything right?" Thus the "I can't" mentality is established.

6. The patient becomes aware that he or she has been functioning from a severely limited self-perception and goes to battle with the voices. (Illustration 4) Powerful Bioenergetic tools are brought to bear in the battle against the parent and the demonic voices, so the Not I, wobbling around on one leg, can be replaced by the true, balanced, grounded self. The parents themselves and their demonic voices are envisioned as being on the bed and are energetically vented against with the use of a tennis racquet. Other ways of expressing fury at the voices can be used as long as the person expresses himself or herself somatically and consequently feels a release from this lifelong bondage.

7. The patient takes the final step—repairing the ego—by repudiating the parent's demonic voice.

Once there has been an emotional release, the soul-self can start to emerge. Enough energy is now available for the person to become aware that he or she is actually separate from the parent and that what the parent said was not true. Since the child has always been too fearful to confront the abusive parent, expressing oneself powerfully and without holding back is vitally necessary. It might sound like this: "I'm not stupid. You're talking about yourself, not me! I'm a conscious human being. I know how to behave. Stop inflicting your generational hatred on me. See me clearly or get out of my life."

The patient usually will feel exhilarated after such an expressive outlet, experiencing a sense of power within that has never been realized before. In time, the patient will be able to diminish the effect of the parental demonic voices and claim an I, an authentic self. I have been witness to the parental demonic voices disappearing altogether.

The time it takes to reclaim the self varies with each person, and each is honored for how he or she moves through the steps of the construct.

However, there is one additional element that is crucial to completing the process: forgiveness.

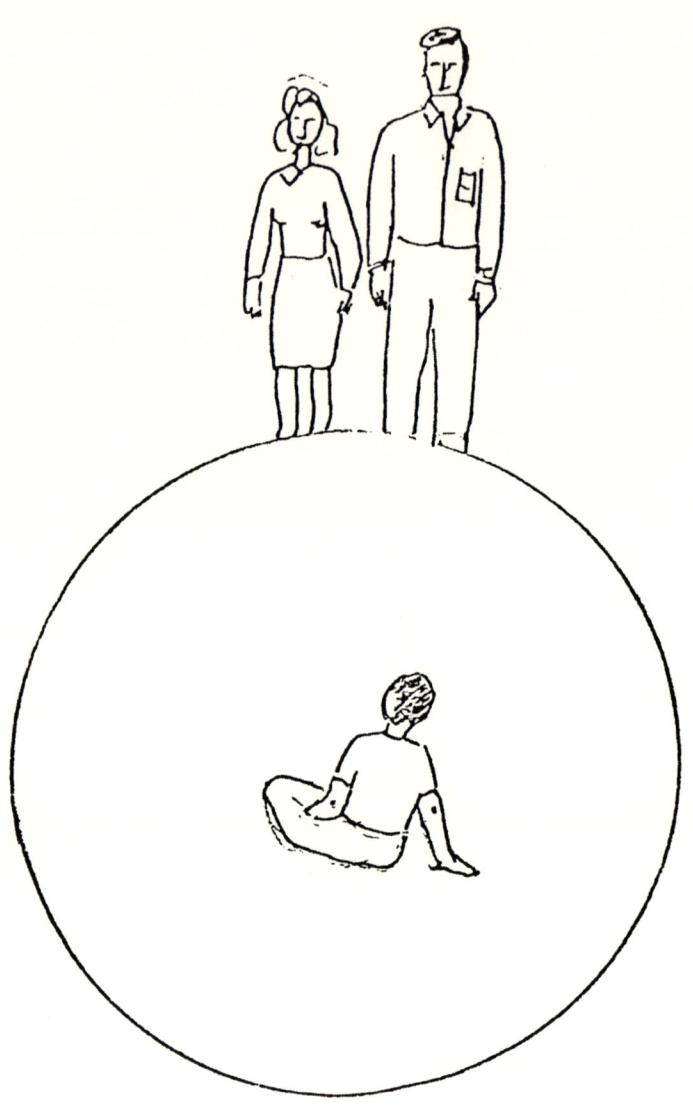

Illustration 1: Parents to Child

Illustration 2: Demon to Child

Illustration 3: Child's Reactions

Illustration 4: Patient to Parents and/or Demon

Chapter 5
Forgiveness: The Ultimate Transformation

I say:

> Forgiveness is not a random concept. It claims
> alignment with your God—a must, an untold honor.
> Vengeance will no longer prevail. The parents did wrong,
> terribly wrong, but do you want to remain connected
> to their savagery?
>
> They know not what they do. They might understand
> in eons of time from now. Will you wait until then,
> arrested in their abuse?
>
> You shake your head. Eradicate the effects
> of their unconsciousness. The abusers are
> satanically possessed. This you know.
> Recognize their evil. Turn the other cheek.
> Let them go. Forgive. Be cleansed and healed
> by a greater wisdom.

God says:

> *Join with me, with my nature, my loves.*
> *I AM THAT I AM. Be your I Am.*
> *Leave no stone unturned, no flower unpicked,*

No tree unclimbed to reach the highest heaven.
Therein I dwell. You can also.
But the density of human thought forgets
The height to which each soul can soar.
I appreciate climbers. I appreciate the serpent too.
I appreciate the man and woman I fashioned
Out of clay who breathe into themselves my breath.
Do not look upon those who bear you
malice--a rugged cross--as enemies,
but rather as humans gone astray,
infiltrated by the Prince whose light
did shine so long ago and who now brings
to my creation misery and alienation from my love.
You believe Lucifer's treachery, flesh of my flesh,
But his ways are so insignificant in contrast
to the ways in which my nature sings.
Let yours sing also. Listening to Luciferian moanings
will waste you and disperse you
from my innermost supply of love and wisdom.
Forgive, loves of my sinews. Forgive even Lucifer,
as I do. In doing so, the delicate, gossamer thread
between you and me will not be broken.
Our natures are one. Did not my Son,
he of my innermost substance, tell this to all:
Forgive them, for they know not what they do?
You do know. Be in tune with the knowing.

FORGIVE!

It is the only way—
for it is mine, and as mine,
it is yours.

ARE WE NOT ONE?

Forgiveness, then, is the transformative process that will bring us into God's realm. Though it is difficult to give up our victimized selves, we must, to be one with ourselves and with him. Separation from God is synonymous with becoming victims of the forces of evil. Those of you who have sought therapy to undo the parental abuses will now understand that when your parents foisted their viciousness on you, their innocent offspring, their dark forces were in operation—and they themselves were victims of the dark forces of their parents.

The therapeutic process unveils the abuses imposed on the child. However, no matter how extensive the therapeutic process is, until the nature of the dark forces is exposed, the person will remain infiltrated.

God's intervention is imperative for all humankind. Through forgiveness, we can transcend our limited nature. Only when man's vengefulness and unforgiving-ness toward others is overcome will fusion with God be possible.

It has been said by Jesus:

> *If ye forgive not men their trespasses,*
> *neither will your Father forgive your*
> *trespasses.*[15]

More can be said, but instead I will quote Nicky Cruz, a renowned Christian evangelist and author of *The Switchblade and the Cross, Soul Obsession, Run Baby Run,* and several other books. In his teenage years, he was a gang leader in one of the worst ghettos in New York City, a drug addict and drug dealer, a murderer—a soul in complete bondage to the satanic forces.

A miraculous transformation took place while he was listening to a preaching evangelist, Pastor David Wilkerson. This evangelist simply told the sneering crowd of teenagers before him, "Jesus loves you."

Nicky Cruz listened, heard, and was inspired. His life was changed. In time he evolved from a state of depravity to living life completely within God's Will, listening to his voice only. He reached a pinnacle of oneness with his I Am wherein forgiveness was an ingredient that he knew was essential for a truthful connection to God. He now knows unequivocally that:

Forgiveness is a gentle and tender kiss from heaven. It is God pressing his lips against a broken heart and kissing away the pain, the sorrow, the shame. Wiping away the hurt forever. He takes a heart filled with regret and replaces it with a new heart—one of hope and joy and love. One that beats strong and true to the music of heaven.

Let God kiss your heart and make it new. Don't live another day of regret. Don't let Satan steal another moment of your future by whispering forgotten memories into your ear . . . let God make you a new creation![16]

Part 3

Gabrielle's and Jesse's Voices in Therapy

INTRODUCTION

It is important to understand when reading the following sections about Gabrielle's and Jesse's voices in therapy that they do not describe the "normal" procedure I engage in with my patients. I will be elucidating only the highlights of the therapeutic process in which the parental demonic and satanic infiltration are emphasized.

Realize, too, that it took both Gabrielle and Jesse a number of years before they were released from their Not I states and entered their I states. Only then were their psyches ready to acknowledge the satanic influences on their lives. Only then were their egos sufficiently developed so that Gabrielle and Jesse could start their journey out of victimization and begin to recognize the evil forces at work in their indulgent patterns of behavior. It is from the egoic state of being that their battle against infiltration took place; and it was from that same I state that their understanding emerged that there is more. Satanic infiltration must be encountered, and beyond that, reaching the I Am state that should be the goal of every human being. This is my goal—for me and for those I treat.

When working with a patient, it is my habit after several sessions to ask him or her to draw a self-portrait. After the usual conflict about the patient's inability to draw has been put in order, I receive a most revealing product. The perceptions are accurate, sensitive, and telling, although so early in the therapeutic experience the patient is unconscious of their significance. You will see revealed in both Gabrielle's and Jesse's portraits a sense of self that was a harrowing and painful starting point for therapy.

Section 1
Gabrielle's Voices in Therapy

CHAPTER 1

When I first met Gabrielle in my waiting room, I was struck by her dark beauty, her slim figure, and her bewildered charm—as well as by her clear blue eyes, which were slightly crossed. Soon I noticed that as she felt more at ease, her eyes would uncross and fix their gaze on mine with a sparkle, while her mouth assumed a warm smile. When she felt safer yet, her eyes darted here and there, scanning the office with wonder and expectation about what the next step might be. I noticed that their expression also exuded a plea for acceptance and love. She seemed to have innate strength even though she seemed unworldly—an innocent victim to the ways of the world.

Is she an angel gone astray in this difficult world? I mused, as I guided her into my office.

From the beginning, Gabrielle was eager to probe and talk to me about her history. After twenty sessions, once our rapport was established and she felt safe and at ease with me, I asked Gabrielle to draw her self-portrait. (Illustration 5) The reader will notice that she looks terrified. Her eyes are almost crossed, as though the horror she was witnessing were unbelievable to her. Her report of her relationship with her mother made it obvious that Gabrielle's demeanor was the result of her mother's wish to kill her in one way or another.

Notice that Gabrielle drew her arms not from the shoulders but from the hips. This reflected her inability—for fear of being destroyed—to reach out to her mother for nurturance as any infant would do. She had never been wanted. Gabrielle perceived her arms and hands as originating from her pelvis not only because her safety was so precarious around her mother, but also because of her father's desperate, confused

Illustration 5: Gabrielle's Self-Portrait

relationship to her, fraught with sexual intentions. At an early age, she had imbibed her father's sexual titillation, which gave her the feeling of being wanted, as well as the security an organism seeks.

Her soul sold out to have such security. I have known patients who displace the nipple of the mother's breast with the man's penis as an organ of nurturance, which results in sexual distortion. In such a situation, the person becomes arrested in an oral phase of development even though she is physically at the genital stage. The phallus becomes a nurturing organ instead of a sexually stimulating one. When Gabrielle reached out to the world, therefore, it was her father she reached out to, feeling infinitely more nurtured and safer than she did when reaching out to her original world—her mother.

Within two years, Gabrielle was able to begin using the construct I had devised to express the effect her parents had on her. As the weeks passed and our sessions continued, I was able to point out the satanic influences and voices that were infiltrating her life. She began by moving through her mother's random comments and their demonic intention that had left her ego severely impaired. Before long, she could distinguish between her parents' demonic voices and Satan's.

CHAPTER 2

The following occurred during the session in which Gabrielle first recognized and responded to the parental demonic voice of her mother, as well as the infiltrating satanic voice that is the true meaning and intention of her mother's words. We began with Gabrielle's recollection of her mother's criticism and rejection:

Mother's Voice: You're no child of mine. They got you mixed up in the hospital. You're olive skinned and have pitch-black hair. We're blond and fair. You don't belong to us. And that nose! Nobody in this family has a beak like you.

Demonic Intention: You're ugly. Different from us. Anyone who is different from us should die. Die. You never should have been born. Besides, you're grotesque.

Gabrielle's Reactions: I'm so ugly. So ugly. My nose is horrible. Who would want to look at me? If I keep my head down all the time, maybe they won't see me and want to hurt me. Oh, my ugly face and nose!

Here are Gabrielle's words, describing the painful stigma she carried about her nose:

> My nose. We all have noses, even the
> animals. The angels—I believe they do,
> too. I have a nose, but for as long as I
> have been living, I've wished I didn't
> have one; or, if I have to have one,
> that it were smaller, more delicate,
> with bone structure so magnificent that

it would make others swoon just by
looking at it.

Once I felt like swooning when I saw
the nose of a worker on the street; he
was raking leaves on the ground as I
stood in front of him. When he turned
his head sideways and I saw his profile,
I believe I did swoon. The straightness
of the features, the delicate curves of
the nostrils, the length of the
protuberance without any error in the
lines of cartilage, ending so naturally,
so appropriately, at the right place
before his lips and chin made their
connections to this beautiful, God-given
appendage. I felt I could stare at it
forever and sing praises to it.

I did that silently until the nose of the
worker became self-conscious and
moved the rest of its body to another
pile of leaves and continued raking. I
was left saddened and bereft.

I entered the house, but stole glances
out of the window, making
unsuccessful attempts to view the
worker's nose from a distance. I heard
him talk to himself, 'She's weird. Does
she think I'm not doing a good job?' I
stopped looking, but kept the image of
his nose in my mind, savoring its
perfection.

I turned to consider my own nose,
not daring to look at it in the mirror, but

simply remembering how it sat
between my cheekbones, above my
lips and chin, connecting to my
forehead. Alas, connecting to my
forehead. This is the problem—too
much protruding bone as it connects to
my forehead. It goes on and on, into
space, almost eclipsing my eyes. My
eyes are beautiful, large, but this
protrusion in front of them is a
distraction—a distraction, indeed, for
the viewer is prevented from looking
into my blue eyes and seeing their
pleading, painful look, begging the
onlooker to see me—*me*. That is, see
me shining through my eyes and not
as my nose.

At my birth, or perhaps while I was still
in the womb, my mother told my
growing protoplasm that I was ugly
and had a large nose. While still in her
womb, I absorbed what she said and
assumed that she must be right. I was
ugly with a large nose, but I would be
born just the same, and she couldn't
stop me. I was determined not to
break my promise to God and his
angels to fulfill my contract with them.
And, so I was born—with a large nose
and ugly. No matter how she tried to
get rid of me, this self and its nose
prevailed and were born.

Gabrielle suffered intensely throughout her life because of her
mother's satanic onslaught. The stigma about her nose and her conviction
that she was ugly grew like a spell that branded her, leaving her in a

state of disconnection from her identity—a Not I state. We see below
how deeply this affected her behavior not just toward herself but with
others as well.

> My nose and I survived, though,
> through many years of life. Most of the
> time I pretended I didn't have a nose.
> This meant I had a black hole between
> my eyes and below my eyes. The
> onlooker would then have to use his or
> her imagination and fill in the space in
> whatever way was needed. This was
> okay with me. Most of my friends and
> acquaintances liked me, so they filled
> in the space with a good-looking
> protuberance.
>
> There were some—not many, but
> some, and there are always some—
> who reacted the same as my mother
> did. I tried to live with their criticism of
> me and my nose, but the voices
> sounded like a rat-a-tat-tat discordant
> holler in my brain and consciousness
> that broke the sound barrier. I had no
> choice but to accept their criticism. And
> when I did, their criticism corroborated
> everything. 'She's right! That witch of
> a mother is right!' I moaned silently.
>
> I would ask others, "Is she right?" They
> would look at me, bewildered.
>
> "Is she right?" I'd scream and run off
> into the distance. I would run
> frantically in the city streets or by the
> ocean if that were possible—run it off,

run it off, run it off . . .

Run what off?

That she was right!

Such was Gabrielle's mother's attitude toward her offspring from the moment of conception. And when the mother's attitude found words, instead of hiding behind her unconscious demonic venom, her full-force intention to destroy came out into the open: mountains broke loose, volcanoes erupted, and lightning struck whenever the mother encountered the energy of her daughter. Gabrielle says:

> And meet we had to. How could I, a
> tot, fend for myself? Where was he, my
> father? Away, away, literally and
> figuratively, away from the horror
> around him. Was he deaf not to hear
> the sadistic slapping sounds of her
> open palmed hand—and sometimes
> each hand—to my face, my chest, my
> shoulders and back?
>
> Was he deaf? What was he doing?
> Looking in front of him at a speck of
> dirt on the floor. He was fixated the
> way a guru would fixate upon the flame
> of a lit candle. He stared upon that
> speck of dirt, most likely hoping to
> reach nirvana—nirvana being his place
> of work on 46th Street where he was
> the boss. Away—just away—from this
> hell.
>
> I continued to feint and parry with my
> opponent, who was now breathing
> heavily. I began to realize that no help

would be coming from my father, who was so very busy—so very busy with his speck of dirt on the floor before him. And so it continued until miraculously, one day, he jumped between the two of us and screamed, "Don't hit her on the head. Not on the head! She might become an imbecile!" He had had a revelation.

I was stunned. 'He loves me!' I thought to myself. 'He loves me!' After that, her slaps became ineffective—like the fluttering of a moth's wings against my body. I smiled at the sudden powerlessness of her assault. 'Love conquers all,' I mused, 'how true!'

Meanwhile my officiator of doom, towering above me, breathed fire from her nostrils and mouth in her last stand against "this mistake" she had given birth to. And then, my mother, the executioner, got tired, spent. She separated herself from her daughter's mutilated carcass. She doused her palms under cold water to ease her aching hands. Then, she patted the family dog lovingly and returned to the kitchen counter to continue cutting the rest of the carrots.

It was over. Silence—an awkward, devastating silence. I stole a glance toward him, still engaged with his speck of dirt on the floor—this enigmatic speck by which he remained mesmerized and . . . safe.

He loves me. My father loves me! were
the sweet illusions that continued to
run around in my brain. I returned to
my school work, but not before I
noticed the smile on her face and read
her mind: 'If she became an imbecile,
she'd be institutionalized. Then I'd be
rid of her.' Her smile broadened.

When I undressed that night, I noticed
that the number of bruises on my body
had multiplied. But I didn't care.

He loves me! My father loves me!

The atmosphere settled into a peaceful serenity as the dog licked the
spot where she had caressed it.

"Oh, Gabrielle," I murmured, wiping away my tears, "Gabrielle..."
She looked at me, her therapist, astonished at my response. She pushed
my compassion aside, and with a hidden, grateful smile, rustled her
papers, her notes for her session, putting them in numerical order. A
sigh, deep and heartfelt, came from her, as she continued to share with
me:

"I was on edge, always on edge. I never knew when the slaps would
come. I never knew what would provoke her. It was horrible. My body
became contracted with fear. I developed an involuntary gesture of
protection whenever she was in my presence: I would place my left arm
against my face and head. She's a demon from hell and the hell became
mine. I became a terrified, beaten-up victim."

I held Gabrielle in my lap. She snuggled close to me, taking in my
warmth. No tears came, just deep sighs. The sighs continued until her
body relaxed, and I could sense she was in a light sleep that took the
edge off a deep exhaustion.

While she was resting, I realized that Gabrielle had nailed it on the head, so to speak. Her mother was a demon from hell and the hell had become Gabrielle's.

She was the daughter of a satanically infiltrated mother. The cruelty of the evil forces at work in a parent who has been overtaken by the dark energy is beyond belief. Gabrielle spoke of her mother's unpredictable mood swings, which, from time to time, alternated with kindness. The neighbors spoke admiringly of the mother's vivacity, charm, and good will toward others and animals. None of these qualities was shown to her daughter, however. Why, then, did she have this unfathomable hatred and rejection of this human being, her own daughter?

Professionals would say, "Schizophrenic behavior." I agree, but not only. "Schizophrenia" labels the disease, but what causes it? Might Gabrielle's mother's nature be inviting the dark spirits to her? Might they be attracted to and feeding upon the self-loathing her mother must have had? Might she be projecting this loathing on Gabrielle and acting from it? Her mother may well be a case of someone in a Not I state, magnetized toward infiltration by the evil forces, and who blames her offspring for her own circumstances.

Gabrielle raised herself from my lap and sat on a chair opposite mine. "That was good," she told me quietly, savoring the precious moments of my caring. She was silent for a moment, and then asked, "How did I remain sane and alive?" Gabrielle was not expecting an answer. "I guess it's my time to overcome," she added. "I'm so committed to moving forward. Perhaps I made this resolution on a soul level before I even came into this life. Maybe that's why I've been able to withstand countless challenges, some of which almost killed me."

"Yes," I agreed, "such as the latest one with Natas, Gabrielle? You can be proud that you are willing to unravel such a profound mystery."

"Well, Dr. A., I'm either stupid or driven by the angels."

"I'd vote for the latter," I told her with great conviction.

Gabrielle sighed more deeply than ever.

CHAPTER 3

When Gabrielle came to her next session a week later, she embraced me strongly and told me how relaxed her body and psyche were following the purging of her mother's voices.

"Even though my I is somewhat muddled, I feel that the most complete aspects of my I are now lying on the epidermal layer of my body. All I have to do is to take a deep breath and push that I out from me with my breath."

I roared with laughter at her imagery and told her to do so—to exhale forcefully to give birth to her I.

Gabrielle's lungs expanded so completely that when she exhaled, I had a sense of being swept away by her breath, and strangely enough I felt as though she had exhaled a live I who stood before the both of us. "Speak to her," I suggested.

"Hello, Gabrielle, my true I. You're really beautiful—dark, and lovely to look at, with a nose that's aquiline but fits into your striking face. I love your body, too. You're me, I'm you, we are one, and I love you," exclaimed Gabrielle. Delighted with her vision, her arms extended so she could bring the image into her and fuse with it.

It took Gabrielle a few minutes before the next revelation occurred: "It's over, Mom," she said thoughtfully. "And as a result of my battle against your voices, the darkness I always felt surrounding you disappeared. That darkness had claws, claws that would hook me and drag me to an abyss. The abyss belongs to you and It.

"Yes, I used to have those thoughts; I still do. But in the past I believed I was crazy to think like that; now, I sense it's the truth. You're possessed, Mom. You sold out a long time ago. I haven't…yet.

"My God, Dr. A., what am I talking about?"

"You're talking about the truth, Gabrielle. Your energy centers are open, especially the one in the center of your forehead—the one that knows everything. You are a child of God; no longer your parents', only his."

Gabrielle smiled, savoring her new self. After a long silence, she asked, "Another scene, Dr. Anneliese? There's more muck to wade through. And now that I have an I, I want to work even harder to make myself available for an I Am. Are you ready?"

I nodded.

I'm a teenager now...

Another teenager, a male, and I have a
date. Ten o'clock is my curfew. We kiss
feverishly on the corner of my block for
the last several minutes before ten.
Out of my right eye, I see my mother's
head jutting out from the fifth-story
window, halfway down the street,
frantically scanning the area for my
whereabouts. I feel the rageful,
paranoid heat from both of them that
far away.

My friend and I bolt down the block
and into the vestibule of my tenement
building.

He wants to kiss some more. So do I,
but my body's stiff with terror. They're
pressing the buzzer relentlessly from
their apartment into the vestibule, as
though the buzzer's energy could
magically fly me up those five flights of
stairs.

"I gotta go," I whisper, tearing myself away from the front of his body, a body so eager, stiff, and expectant. "I gotta go now." That moment taught me what it's like for passion to be torn apart by terror.

I bolt up the stairs—two, three steps at a time. The door is open, and I enter. They stand rigid, accusatory—in their nightshirts—much like the Gestapo in their uniforms.

"What were you doing with this boy? You had sex, didn't you? Take off your clothes. I'll find out if you did or didn't."

Luckily, my hero father stopped her from ripping off my clothes. Out of the blue, he threw himself into a chair, moaning, unable to get his breath, his hand over his heart. She rushed to his side to take care of him.

Was he pretending or was his pain real? I do remember that whenever the word "sex" came up, it turned his nature into a Knights Templar about to rescue a virginal maiden.

More moans. His pain did seem real. She massaged his chest. His "uuhs" and "aahs" were ecstatic. I watched. I guess everybody needs to be touched.

Something's phony, though, I thought.

Was his feverish brain on a rescue
mission to compensate for some
monumental violation many years ago
of my private rights as a human being?
Rights that were mine no matter what
my age? Do I remember what it was?"
I wonder.

"Sure I do! His molestation of my
child's body!"

"Does Gabrielle remember?" he asked
himself. "Out of the question," his brain
told him. "She was too young. Besides
I didn't do it for real; she was too little
for that. But I was desperate. My wife
wouldn't give it to me, so I had to do
something!"

"Yeah," I thought, "you had to do
something. Creep!

"What you did is you despoiled me for
the rest of my life—that's all!" I stalked
off to bed, leaving them in their
melodrama in the kitchen, which had
become a courtroom for sentencing
their daughter.

As I slipped into my nightgown, I
wondered how much longer I'd have to
endure this circus. No! not a circus—
this constant, terrifying walk to the gas
chamber!

I sat back and waited. Gabrielle remained calm, calmness she adhered
to ferociously, as though she were gripping a log in the ocean with all

her strength after a shipwreck. She was a weather-beaten survivor; the glimmer of light in her soul never forsaking her. When she finally reacted, she said:

"I feel tainted—rotten in my genitals. My father molested a tot." She shook her head. "And I can't relate to a man in a real way. I don't trust them. Either I withhold or I give everything to them, hoping they're honest with me and love me. My mother's voices are always there, and they sure don't help.

Mother's Voice: You'll never get a decent man. Who would want you? Who would want a rotten mess like you?

Demonic Intention: Whore! Disgusting whore!

Gabrielle's Reactions: I am a whore. I've behaved like a whore—look at my escapades with Jesse and with Natas. I'll do anything to be loved and accepted. I'll take money, because I can't make ends meet. God, I'm a mess. She's right!

Gabrielle sat in her chair, slumped over her knees, defeated—a Not I in its most vulnerable and lost state. Her mother's voices had once again swallowed up her I.

I pondered what to do next. Nothing I could say to her while in such a condition could persuade her to move out of it, so deeply ensconced was she in her misery. Finally, I circled around her chair and screamed at her:

"Your mother's right, Gabrielle. You are a whore. You behave like one. And you're an irredeemable mess. Therapy can't help you. No one can. Give up!"

After a while, I noticed her back rise to an erect position in the chair. She looked around to see where I was. I knew enough to be securely standing behind my desk. Her eyes were fierce, her jaws protruded. She looked like a tigress, ready to spring toward me. I emphatically pointed to the bed and the tennis racquet, tools she had used throughout her therapeutic process with me. I needed to shift this energy away from me and what I had said and redirect it to the bed and tennis racquet. A part of her consciousness understood, and she dashed toward the bed and grasped the racquet in her hand. Her rage erupted:

> You bitch! bitch! You knew what was
> going on. You didn't give it to your
> husband because you're a frozen, heartless
> cunt. You hate sex. I don't and that doesn't
> make me a whore. I'm mixed up because
> my genitals aren't mine. They're his—your
> husband's. I feel married to him even though
> he's an asshole. You're jealous of me and
> always were. You're the ugly one with a
> beak, not me! Others think I'm beautiful.
> In time, I'll think so, too. I'll get this issue
> straightened out.

> I feel like a whore because
> I listened to you all of my life. But all I want
> is love—a healthy love—not the love you have with
> your wimpy spouse. I want a love that's honest, where
> two people talk to each other, and make love with
> God in it. For a while I thought I had that with Jesse.

Then Gabrielle threw the racquet on the bed and burst into grunts while grinding her teeth, as though she wanted to tear her mother apart. I gave her a towel to bite into; then she twisted it with her hands as though she were wringing her mother's neck. She stomped on the towel representing her mother's body, screamed at it, and finally kicked it to the other end of the office. She was spent, but she rushed to me to be held. I did so until all her feelings abated and she breathed normally.

"Your life was in danger, Dr. A.," she told me, laughing with much zeal and glee at her power.

"I know," I told her, "but this was a danger I invited. It liberated you."

"It sure did."

CHAPTER 4

"And now, Gabrielle, it's time to look at how you can extricate yourself from feeling like a whore. Your father's act of molestation is one of depravity, perpetrated by the evil forces. It doesn't matter that his wife, your mother, was, as you put it, a cold cunt and wouldn't satisfy him sexually. It's a satanic act that he sponsored with the help of the dark forces and that affected you adversely all of your life up to now.

"To you, love means giving your body over to sex, as you did with your father at a very young age. You wanted his love, not his sex, but in order for you to have an ally against your mother, you succumbed to his aberrant need. Most of the time, he betrayed you with his affections. Therefore, you approach men with this twisted psyche, always hoping that love will be forthcoming. You sought this with Natas, the fallen angel of this universe, or in human terms—a fallen man like Jesse was when you met him.

"The dark forces know the effects of molestation on a child's psyche. They know that the child will be tainted, confused, unable to love, and consequently become prey to their attacks. Such a child will forever be looking for the father's missing, heartfelt love for his offspring. As adults, women or men will forever reach out to the wrong partners, looking for that early fulfillment that no other adult peer will be capable of or want to give them.

"You must purge yourself of your father's sexual depravity, Gabrielle, so that love will fill your heart and your I self can be in charge of what you draw in to satisfy you."

"I'm beginning to feel hopeless again, Dr. A."

"I understand, but that's not my intention, Gabrielle. I'm trying to move you out of satanically infiltrated feelings about yourself to your true I. You had glimpses of this self in the last session.

"You rightfully expressed your rage at your mother for her satanic behavior toward you, but I don't hear any protestations coming from you toward your father. He was your lifeline: his passivity gave you the semblance of being a father-friend. But when you objectify him, how do you understand his relationship to you?"

Gabrielle thought for a few moments and then responded, "Like a passive wimp under her domination. He'll do anything she wants him to, even kill me." As she listened to her own words about her savior, her father, Gabrielle became almost catatonic.

"What you just admitted takes courage, Gabrielle," I told her, holding her hands firmly in mine.

"I guess I don't want to look at him realistically, because if I'm disgusted by him I'll have no one. Illusionless Gabby, alone in the world…Maybe that's why I look for love in men and sex. It's like I hear a voice telling me, 'You're entitled to get it and feel good. Do it. Just one more time. The last time. Don't even think about not doing it.' In a flash I'm 'doing it, but, when it's over and I'm abandoned once again, the orgasm fix makes me want to kill myself.

"I never realized until now that my parents' evil voices have taken over so fully. I feel tainted worse than ever. This self-loathing is just devastating. I can feel myself falling into my Not I state.

She looked so small and dejected, but even so, I could see arising in her the beginnings of a new strength in the midst of her struggle. "Dr. A., I don't want to sell myself short anymore—whether it's with men or the voices. I want to be me. I know what's right and wrong, but often I don't do what I know is right. At decision time, I'm taken over by a whirlwind that comes from nowhere and sweeps me into its vortex."

"You've begun to recognize satanic infiltration into your psyche, Gabrielle. That infiltration happens when a person is lazy, indulgent, and unwilling to face the necessary truth of their own cancerous negative thoughts, feelings, images from which they are living life. These cancerous-thought seeds multiply, feeding verdant soil where the evil spirits of this world can take hold and penetrate the being. When they exist in one's self without an accompanying consciousness—as they do in your parents—the havoc is severe indeed, setting a person, such as you, on the path toward evil."

"But I've worked so long and so hard on myself," Gabrielle retorted, clearly exasperated.

"You have, Gabrielle. Realize, however, that persistence after the truth is not the criterion with which most of us humans live our lives. We're flawed and we become lazy, moaning from victimization about how long and how often we've gone to battle with the voices; and we pride ourselves on our efforts. We ask, 'But why does there have to be more? Why do I have to give up my illusions—about my father, my nose, my inability to love?'"

"That's not fair," pouted Gabrielle. "I'm doing the best I can."

"Have you really done the best you can, Gabrielle?" I asked, holding back a grain of impatience. "Might you be succumbing to the grandiosity that sometimes accompanies a therapized self?"

When I observed her pout increasing, I suggested, "Let's look at the problem with your nose and your so-called ugliness, all of it foisted on you by your mother. Why haven't you mastered this voice, even though you have a great deal of consciousness about the matter?"

"I don't know," she sputtered, taken by surprise. "Maybe it's because I've never approached the problem like a deep-sea diver, going into the depths of the ocean or going deep into my unconscious. It seems like I've destroyed her a million times on the bed, Dr. Anneliese, and the trauma has lessened, but I admit that this particular voice still haunts me. Why? Does God want to torture me personally because I've been a whore and allowed Natas into my life—in short, sold out?"

"Gabrielle, if we look at the life of St. Paul, who was a murderer before he was endowed by the Holy Spirit, we will realize that it is our state of mind, heart, and soul that needs changing. And the change happens because we want to change, we want another consciousness, we want to listen to God's voice, not the voice of the ungodly. We want our true Self; we want to be reunited with that Self which of course refers to the God within us. In other words, we want wholeness.

"But infiltration happens. Our consciousness has to become diligent about such a reality. St. Paul was. Why can't you be?"

Gabrielle looked at me strangely, wondering if she had the strength of a St. Paul.

"You ask why, Gabrielle," I continued to question her, hoping to nullify her doubts. "That's the beginning of receiving an answer."

"Yeah," I've been asking why constantly, but I don't get answers. So, I feel rejected by God and hate him."

"Most of humanity is angry at God for myriad reasons. We either have parental transferences to God or we hate him because we believe he cast us out of heaven unjustifiably; we wanted to stay in heaven forever, avoiding our struggles on Earth or we wanted to be his favorite like Lucifer did. It's difficult to accept that we aren't his favorite, so we betray God and we betray the divine in us for centuries. Whatever the reasons, we've become separated from our Source. We are tempted and unwittingly succumb to Satan."

Gabrielle listened carefully, but I could see she was irritated. "But so many people seem to get along playing Satan's game. They get involved in loveless sex, drugs, dishonesty—all of that stuff. They don't work on themselves for years and years as I have, and they don't have the pain I've had."

"Look more closely, Gabrielle, and you'll see that in many cases the psyche is invaded but the person doesn't know it. There's an odor of putrefaction around those people; they're masked and speak from voices that are alien to who they really are. Possession might very well have taken place."

"You scare me when you say that. I don't want to be possessed. I've been through that."

"If you don't want that and you meant what you said earlier in the session about working harder than ever to grow into your I Am, then close your eyes now and let me bring the Angel of Truth into the room. This angel, like all angels, is a supernatural entity originating from heaven. It surrounds those who are willing to seek its help and tells the person a truth that is not ordinarily accessible. I'll invoke it in the language of the Spirit. If you allow the Holy Spirit to penetrate your heart and soul, it will lift encrusted debris from your psyche. You'll become aware of how invaded you still are by the dark forces, who feast on unresolved patterns, creating your worst nightmares."

"Okay, Dr. A., I'm ready…sort of," she said apprehensively.

Within a minute, the sounds of the supernatural language of the Spirit brought a sweeping, cleansing vibration into the room that settled around us both. It took Gabrielle a while to release herself from her resistant state and surrender to the angel's presence.

Then she said, "I feel a vibration coming around my body; it's like sea water lapping onto the shore. It feels strange but compelling. There's a murmur that's hard to understand. It's getting clearer and closer…Oh, no. It's an ugly voice, Dr. A. It's horrible, menacing."

SATANIC VOICE

> Pinocchio. Woodpecker. Ha ha ha! Take your beak and file it on the bark of trees. That's all you're good for. Therapy's a crock. You'll be penniless, and where will it get you? Listen to me. Advice is free. You'll get it all for nothing. I'll help you, but you've got to do as I say. No pain like in therapy or asking God who answers in his own time. God's too busy. I'm always available. I'm predictable. And the goodies you'll get are real. Remember? Jewelry, sex, love, limousines, great clothes, a mansion to live in…

Gabrielle looked dazed. "Is that voice real?" she asked me. "'Do I remember?' it asked. Only too well. Wasn't I in a hospital with a miscarriage? This is weird! I thought I'd gotten rid of the voices. Why are they still plaguing me? Why do I have to remember the episode with Natas? Haven't I been through enough suffering and guilt? When will I be able to take it easy and not probe endlessly, always anxious?"

"Gabrielle, the Earth is a laboratory for working on your unwanted, accumulated baggage. Take the opportunity to do that. At least, for right now, tell that satanic voice to get away from you or else you'll remain in a pattern of victimization, whining, 'Poor me, I've had it so hard.' If you remain in such a pattern, they'll invade and take possession."

"Then let them. I'm tired! Tired! I've given it my best shot. Nothing's good enough for you!" she belted out at me, looking away toward the floor, reminding me of her father's speck of dirt on the floor.

I tried again to reach her: "Gabrielle, an unworked pattern can be likened to a deliberate walk into hell. Once in hell, there's no recourse but to surrender. Or, you can fight and face it—face the pattern directly, with all of its desperate pain."

"I'm an orphan. I have no one. I can't do it! I can't take any more," Gabrielle shouted, whirling her gaze from the floor into my face. "Do you hear? I can't, don't want to. I wanna rest. Rest, Dr. Anneliese. Do you hear? I've gotta go!"

She thrust her arms into her coat and bolted out the door, slamming it behind her. I sat, shocked. I hadn't anticipated her outburst. I was deeply upset and questioned myself thoroughly about what I might have done differently. I prayed that she would find her way. I didn't know if I would ever see her again.

CHAPTER 5

Two years passed before Gabrielle called for another session. When I beheld her, I noticed that she had changed. She looked gaunt, irritable, and anxious. She had been struggling with her satanic voices, with life, and with her path to the truth—these challenges were everyday occurrences. In catching me up on her life, she informed me that her father had died soon after her last session with me.

"Did the situation improve after your father's death?" I asked innocently, thinking that some closeness might have developed between Gabrielle and her mother.

Gabrielle was flabbergasted by my question. "Are you serious, Dr. Anneliese? Why and how should things change?"

She was bitter and sarcastic throughout the session, and she needed to relate almost compulsively about the events of her life during her absence from therapy. It was as though she had a script from which she was speaking—a dramatic, thought-out, yet spontaneous script that became her soliloquy. I listened and was silent:

> He was dead, dead, dead as dead as
> can be. She remained vicious, vicious,
> vicious, and satanic. Nothing changed
> her nature. She looked around like a
> frantic bug whose nest had been
> destroyed.
>
> "Poor me!" she wailed. "Look at what
> he did—he died, and left me all alone."

She eyed me, her imbecile daughter.
Gabrielle is someone who knows the
world, she thought. I gave her a home,
food on the table, tolerated her
existence. I never disowned her or
threw her out. She owes me, now that
I'm alone and needing.

The shoe's on the other foot, mother of
mine, I thought but didn't say. I owe
you nothing but my hatred of you,
because you are a wretched, wretched
soul. I visit you as little as decorum
permits. When I'm forced to visit, my
guts turn into twisted ropes. I become
infiltrated by your pervading demons,
which are relentless in their pursuit of
me.

Stay away from me! I'm still coping
with the past I endured. Your brutality
sticks in my brain and body. How do I
eradicate you from my soul? God help
me! What must I do?

A voice then entered my lonely state. I
was bewildered, but I listened. Its
sweetness and gentleness soothed my
heart. It said:

*FORGIVE! Move forward. Be guided by
us.*

Forgive? I thought, forgive when voices
like the following rant on relentlessly, invading
me completely?

You're really an ugly, stupid thing,
unworthy of giving a home to. Work for
your living.

Don't bother me. It's my turn to be
taken care of. I gave birth to you. That
was enough. I loved our dog more than
you. I married your father because of
you and lived this life of torment. You
were my mistake—now pay for it. You
owe me half of your paycheck; other
than that, don't visit me except on
holidays—so I can keep face with the
neighbors.

I'd rather die than visit you, woman of
Satan's design. You made your bed. Lie
in it. Learn what injustice you meted
out and suffer as does my shipwrecked
nature.

Right now you're dying from cancer of
the breasts—a fitting disease for what
you have sown. I'll get you into a
nursing home, a favor to you by which
my obligation ends. Do I feel
compassion? No, I don't! What I feel is
sadness and hatred, that's all.

She died soon after and she's probably
in hell. I wonder, are you out of my
psyche? No. Death didn't do it—then
what will? She's stuck in me like Krazy
Glue, and Krazy Glue holds on
relentlessly. What must I do to rid
myself of her? Forgiveness? What does
forgiveness entail? My heart is stone-

cold dead. How can I manufacture
forgiveness of her?"

And then, one morning after my
soliloquy of detestation, I went into
the street. I tripped on the curb right onto
my nose, which broke into many
pieces—this nose that she had
ridiculed. How strange, I thought, that
I should fall on the protuberance I, too,
have grown to abhor.

I was bloodied and disfigured for many
weeks—enough time to contemplate
the event. Out of that time came
another tale, one that is worth telling.

Gabrielle barely paused for breath before she continued:

One night I dreamed a significant
dream instigated by the angels. I saw
my mother's face: She was plaintive,
remorseful—begging me to forgive her
abuses. I was shocked and bewildered.
I wondered, is this a demonic tease or
can I believe her plea?

She'd been dead for more than a year;
yet hateful outbursts, demonic
thoughts were still reverberating in my
brain. What shall I do? I thought in
great agitation. I'll take a chance and
listen to her, although trusting her is a
dangerous undertaking.

I asked:

"Was it you who made me trip and fall a few days ago?" She gave no response; instead, she turned away. Then as though prompted by the Lord himself—she said most sorrowfully, "Yes, it was I, and the demons that possess me. When I saw your pain and your disfigurement, I realized I was being vengeful. Then something happened: My heart opened suddenly and I begged my demons to leave you alone. They left, and I've been so much freer ever since. A sweet angel whom I speak to on a daily basis, who flutters around me to give me counsel, must have guided my way of handling the situation, knowing you and I want rectification."

I looked at her incredulously. Her plea was long overdue. "I'm not ready to give you forgiveness," I told her with an edge of bitterness. "Perhaps when my nose and body are healed, I'll feel more receptive to your request."

She nodded, disappointed. She went on her way—back to hell where she resided.

Her angel told me, "Be patient, child. This is all she can muster. As for you, are you readier than she, or do you need more compassion?"

I truly had thought I was ready to forgive and be forgiven, but when I

faced the truth in myself, I understood
I was eaten up by victimization. I was
unconsciously betraying myself. Her
satanic voices were real, no question of
that—voices with horrible judgments.
But who would I be without their cruel
chatter? They've become my beacon of
who I am. I have been living in
illusions—as an infinitesimal fraction of
God's intentions.

Why do I continue this sabotage of my
nature? Inwardly I believe that the
demonic voices are right: I should be
able to perceive my reality more
clearly; instead, I rely on
rationalizations that neutralize my
pain: She doesn't mean what she is
saying. Others think I'm beautiful. But
her comments stick like burrs in my
heart until I live my life from them.
Why does my unconscious collude with
such distortion? Lack of faith, I guess.
I have to believe in something. My
mother didn't want me nor did God. Or
so I thought.

Satan always has been waiting—
waiting—waiting with its embracing
energy. It was something, somebody,
someone. It accepted me and I no
longer was alone.

With much more probing, it dawned
upon my psyche that she had foisted
upon my nose and the rest of me all
her heart's hatred reaped from her evil
father.

'Aha!' I thought, 'here is the truth, the larger truth of this matter. It is exponential continuing from generation to generation.

'Then why does it continue?' I wondered to myself. The answers came quickly. I was lazy, too indulgent, too mesmerized by victimization—all qualities that create ripe soil for infiltration by those rapacious, bloodthirsty vipers.

She appeared to me again another night. It was as though she were transmitting a confessional that conveyed to me how miserable her life had been—the loss of her own mother, and a sadistic father, who constantly taunted his children.

He married again, but life was no better. The new, young wife fought him valiantly. "I became pregnant with you," she explained self consciously, "and married a man I had to marry. It was better than remaining at home.

"I was young, not too conscious, unaccustomed to a bulging belly. The pregnancy was disastrous—too much, too soon. I was inundated by my inherited hatred of life. Satan overtook my brain and dictated what I must do: that is, to get rid of you. You were not aborted from my womb, however, much as I tried. Your insistence to be born prevailed. You know the rest.

"I am truly sorry, innocent being; forgive me. I beg you honestly to have compassion—my heart is heavy with this burden. I want to be freed from hell; I want another life and the chance to make amends. Forgive me, daughter. I have nothing more to say."

"I hear you, Mamma," mumbling this word as though I were stumbling on rocks. "I need just a while longer. It's important to forgive you, to separate completely. Then my voices will be severed from the demons, and my heart will connect to God. Come tomorrow. We'll speak."

And now, I wish to converse with the Lord:

I forgave you, my beloved.
Do as I have always done.

Seven times seventy
is a speck of compassion in
our realm.

All humans make mistakes.
Forgiveness helps them rectify,
But be certain you are honest
yourself.

True forgiveness keeps
your wings steadfast—

an angel without fault.

When you are ready
there will be no error,
no recriminations,
nor a falling back.

Forgive.
Do as I do.

When Mamma returned, I told her
triumphantly, "I'm ready."

She smiled, tears dropping from her
eyes. She whispered gratefully, looking
earnestly into my face:

"Thank you, Gabrielle."

I was speechless. "Gabrielle, Gabrielle," was all I could say, at a loss
to express myself. I embraced her, even though her body was stiff and
cold from anguish, mostly noticeable when I took her hands in mine. I
was deeply impressed by her heartfelt effort to overcome the monstrous
experiences of her life.

She released her hands from mine and sat in her usual seat opposite
me.

"Thanks, Dr. Anneliese, but all this happened because of you. In my
two-year absence, I carried your teachings around with me, like Rosary
beads. What would Dr. A. think and do? I'd ask myself. It worked,
but I'm not out of the woods. I'm back because the voices are shouting
at me maniacally—as though they own me. I try to turn them off by
hitting them on the bed, which helps; but after I stop, they return more
intensified.

"You were right about unfinished business becoming a pattern that
they prey upon without mercy. It's dawned on me, too, that there's a step
missing, and I need help with it. I'm in a place similar to the one I was in

when I left two years ago. I thought I could do the next step—whatever it is—by myself, but I can't. Help me, please."

I was both terrified and ecstatic with her progress. Terrified because the satanic forces were actively engaged in her psyche and determined to destroy her; this happens when a person is most ready to move out of his or her darkness. I was ecstatic because Gabrielle was on the brink of extraordinary realizations. My body was shivering from excitement and my desire to move her forward. I went to work.

CHAPTER 6

"Close your eyes, Gabrielle," I instructed her, "while I call on the Angel of Truth. This angel will elicit any satanic forces around you, which you then can eradicate."

A few minutes elapsed during and after the sounds of the spiritual language again filled the room. Then the satanic voice presented itself. It sounded like this:

SATANIC VOICE:

> You're back with 'that therapist?' We had you ensnared. You were too scared to be alone in the world, now that they're both dead. Your mother's with us. Your father's hovering in-between. But, you're the one we want. Don't you want to be together with them on the other side—a happy family?
>
> She wants you to come. So does he. He'd really make love to you, now that you're grown up, beautiful, and sexy. Come on, it's easier than therapy. You'd live in a grand place with me, as my assistant. After all, we've known one another from before. We were good together, weren't we? It would be even better this time; I'll give you more than before.
>
> Say yes to me, your Gamiel. Think of it: no more pain, no more suffering, no more penny-pinching. All you want will be at your fingertips. A sweet yes will make it so.

Gabrielle: "Oh. Dr. Anneliese, I get so confused. Natas knows exactly how to get to my weakest places. Its voice is so mesmerizing. Oh, to be wanted, accepted, and loved—I want all of it so much. How long can I live without having those basic feelings in my life? Natas has found my greatest vulnerability. I could float away into love, acceptance, and being wanted. I need every ounce of strength not to give in."

"I know, Gabrielle, but go to the bed and destroy this force that doesn't want your good. Throw it off your body and psyche. Fight it off!"

Gabrielle whined, "I'm tired, tired. I've been doing this for two years. Facing the demons has sapped me of my energy and will. I feel raw—so vulnerable."

Dr. Anneliese: Fight! Ask for help!

Gabrielle: (in a whimper, while hitting the bed repeatedly) I'm fighting.

Dr. Anneliese: Call upon someone for help.

Gabrielle: I am. You!

Dr. Anneliese: I'm here. Besides me.

Gabrielle: I don't know. God? Will he listen?

Dr. Anneliese: Ask!

Gabrielle: I'll try.

Dr. Anneliese: Do it!

Gabrielle: God, God, I call upon you—even though I've shunned you, hated you, even reviled you. Save me from that enemy who is your worst foe as well as mine. Help me defeat it. I want your love; not its. Its attention is rotten, evil. I know this without doubt. I've learned painfully, but unmistakably. Help me! Hear me! Cleanse me! I want to return to you. I have that right; I'm your creation. Take me back!

Gabrielle fell on her knees, her head on the bed, heaving convulsive sobs and murmuring the same invocation repeatedly until she was drained and near collapse.

Suddenly a peaceful atmosphere replaced the former turbulence. The room became sweetly effervescent with a supernatural energy pervading it. Both Gabrielle and I felt it, and we both sensed the words that then emerged:

> I hear you, my beloved. Be at peace.
> Know that I am your Father and your
> Mother—your true love. Natas has
> retreated and will no longer haunt you
> now that I am present. Lucifer will always
> tempt you, but your love for me will
> deter It. Your love for me will always
> protect you, guide you, and keep your
> path straight.

Gabrielle: Say your words again and again, Lord. Again and again!

᧞

A long silence followed. Gabrielle listened intently, hoping for more revelations to be given her. She finally turned to me, glowing with satisfaction, and said:

> AMEN.

The tears rolled down our cheeks as we embraced hard, quietly ecstatic. After a long time, we moved apart and sat in silence, unwilling to change the atmosphere and move to the next moment. Gabrielle did first. She whispered:

> I am re-formed.
> I am re-grown.
> I am re-born.

I heartily concurred:

> AMEN.

Section 2
Jesse's Voices in Therapy

CHAPTER 1

Jesse sat in my waiting room for the first time six months after Gabrielle's initial visit. Neither of them knew that I was the psychotherapist for the other. Jesse had been sent to me by a female social worker who became acquainted with him in a drug rehabilitation center. She knew of my work with people who were struggling with satanic infiltration; when he was free from drugs, she referred him to me for psychological work.

When I approached Jesse as he thumbed nervously through a magazine in the waiting room, I was witness to a handsome blond, trim, blue-eyed man in his late thirties. I extended my hand to him, which he took into his. He shook it vigorously—so vigorously that I could feel the grasping need in his handshake. I sensed that he wanted to jump into my lap to be held and protected. When I withdrew my hand after a while, he was startled and drew back with an apology: "Sorry, I didn't mean to hurt you."

I ushered him into my office. He settled into a chair opposite mine. I then asked him to tell me why he had made this appointment. The following information unfolded:

After he was dismissed from his film work, he spent two miserable years living in the streets, as both a drug addict and a drug dealer. When the police got on his trail, he began to realize what a dangerous life he was living. However, it was only when destiny created a serendipitous event in his life that he awakened to his dreary reality. One day a fellow druggie asked him whether he knew of someone called Jesse Jason.

"Maybe…why?" replied Jesse, cagily.

"I just saw a film in which the star reminded me of you. Now, don't get a swelled head. You're kinda beat up to be a film star. But, it puzzled me and I thought I'd ask you. Your name is Jesse, too, just like the star. You never know how far a person can fall."

With those seemingly benign comments, the druggie left, and Jesse felt as though an atom bomb had been dropped on him. 'I'm too beat up to be a film star, the guy told me!' thought Jesse. "Oh yeah?" he said out loud.

He quickly headed for the men's room in a shelter he frequently slept in. He had noticed a full-size mirror there, but had always avoided looking at himself in it. This time, he approached the mirror, but tentatively, cautiously, fearing that the guy was right. He was alone, so he took his time with what felt like a painful, surgical procedure. First he approached his image sideways. It's not that bad considering I'm out of shape, he mused. The biggest challenge for him was to look at his body and his face frontward. He did so, all the while squinting his eyes so that the contours of his face and body remained fuzzy. He tried again, his eyes now open wider.

Unexpectedly, another homeless man came into the room. Jesse, not wanting to look weird with his eyes wide open took a fast look in the mirror at his own front—his body, his face, then all of himself. He let out a screeching howl: "G...O...D!" and ran out of the men's room, looking as though he had seen Lucifer itself.

This marked the end of his old life and the beginning of another way of living. Jesse abruptly stopped selling drugs, entered a rehabilitation center, and sought therapeutic help.

In the telling of his story, Jesse the actor had emerged: alive, expressive, imaginative, and humorous. He mimed his actions until we were both doubled over with laughter. The unfamiliarity between us had lifted, and we unhesitatingly began our work together.

CHAPTER 2

As I had done with Gabrielle, after a few weeks in therapy I asked Jesse to draw a self-portrait, which is shown on the following page. (Illustration 6) When I observed the product, I wondered whether he had understood me correctly. I was baffled because his drawing of himself was a blown-up box that had little resemblance to the person sitting before me.

I asked him for an explanation, and he told me, "When I was fired from my film job, my psyche did a flip-flop. As you now know, I became a homeless drug addict and drug dealer—a mess, a ne'er do well. I was becoming the epitome of my father's voice, which always told me that I was nothing and that I didn't exist. These voices took over until I felt as though I was slowly becoming him. He weighed 350 pounds, ate incessantly, and probably was never sexually potent. These days, I'm not having sex either. When I'm lucid, I wonder about my sexuality, but I push the matter away, blaming everything on my mixed-up state.

"Like my father, I shove food into my mouth as though it would solve all problems. When I was a star, I took care of my body, watched my diet, and I had massages. I would rather have died than look anything like him. Recently, I've become aware of what a powerful effect his psyche has on me—even though he's been dead since I was a young adult. It's horrible how quickly I've taken on his loathsome image and how his voices are undoing me even today."

I was delighted with Jesse's insights and I acknowledged, "They have been finding you fertile ground to contaminate." I knew he was ready and willing to recognize and disentangle himself from a horrific past. On the surface, Jesse's body looked proportionate except for a slight deformity

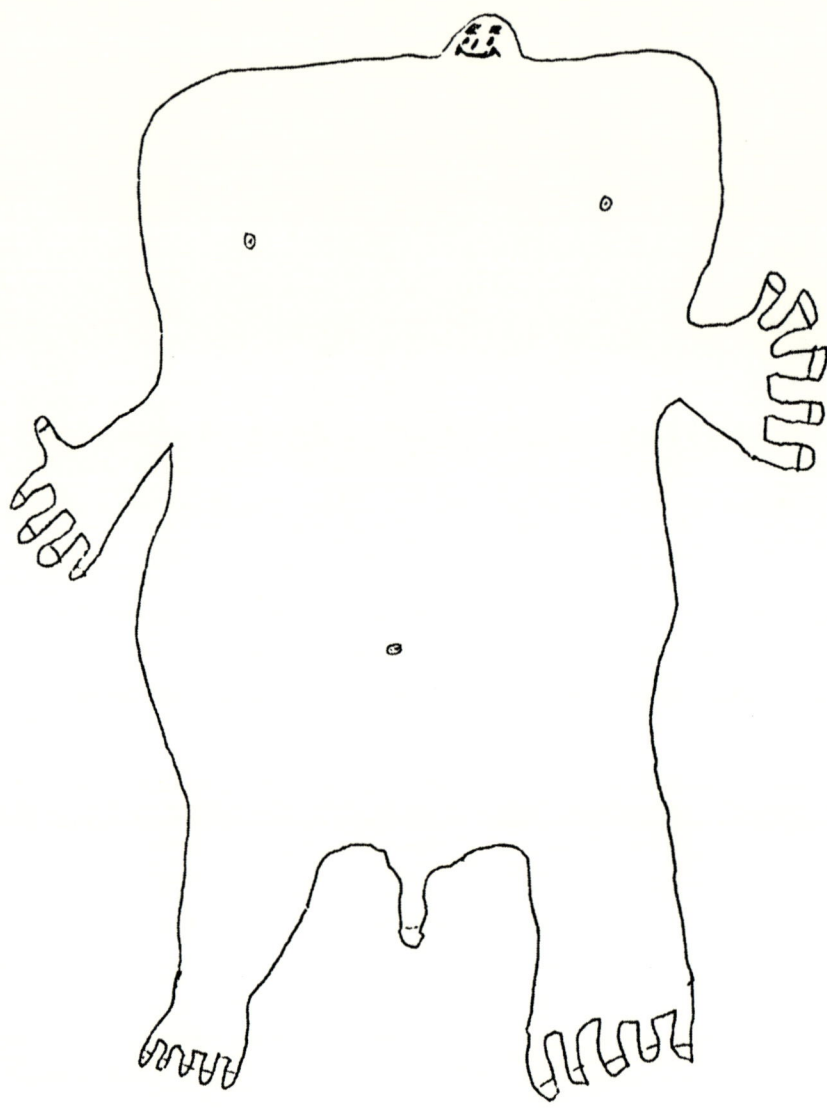

Jesse's Self-Portrait

around his shoulder girdle and arms, which appeared foreshortened because, when he was an infant, his mother's unavailability stunted the normal, reaching, developmental gesture of an infant and child. His chest cavity appeared contracted and young; his body was spastic and filled with fear; and his sexuality was deeply disturbed. From the world's perspective, however, Jesse could have been a fashion model.

I could tell that Jesse was enthusiastic about moving ahead and was going to be easy to work with. I looked forward to the next meeting.

As Jesse's history unfolded in therapy, it became clear that his father's voice was the prime force behind Jesse's low self-esteem, which consequently made him so vulnerable to the evil voices. As soon as I felt that Jesse was becoming aware enough to discern and stand up to the parental demonic voice of his father, I encouraged him to do so.

Father's Voice: I can't help you now with your homework. I don't have time for you. You're in my way.

Demonic Intention: You're a dumb shit, not worth bothering about. I wish you'd never been born.

Jesse's Reactions: I'm bad. I'm not worth bothering about. I'll just be quiet and not make a sound. I'll be a good boy. Maybe then he'll love me.

Father: I'm not sure I should have gotten married. If I had known that your mother, you, and your brother would cause me so much aggravation, I would have had second thoughts. Go to your mother, you rotten kid. I wish I could disappear and do what I want to do.

Jesse's Reactions:

> I feel unwanted.
> Nevertheless I'm born.
> Finally I'm out of that womb.
> The air is cleaner, purer—
> mine, not hers.
> In time, though, I learn that
> everything is hers or his,
> not mine . . . theirs.
> She's warm, but anxious; she's
> sort of loving. He's BIG, his mouth

chewing, chewing constantly
like an animal with its feed.

I'm afraid to get near him.
I'm afraid he'll eat me up,
swallow me whole, then spew
me out like vomit in the streets,
the streets of Brooklyn where
I was born.

He's a busy man, too busy for his son.
"You have a son," the nurse said when
his wife's last shrieks had bounced
against the hospital walls.

"Who me? A son? I'm the son. I'm the
sun," he dazedly replied to all who
stood around me.

"Ha ha ha," they cackled in disbelief.
"He's not serious."

"But, he is," I insisted with my
toothless, not-yet-speaking-but-
knowing soul. "He is! And that will
shape my malehood—balls, heart, belly
and all. A son-drenched father who is
burning up with rage that his precious
seed inside my mother's womb gave
birth to someone else but him. To be
born again and again was his desire:
the eternal child who would be just
born forever. He had a son, but who
would even know it. It was up to her to
raise this loved but unloved effigy.

I was handsome, they all agreed. From time to time he looked upon my face, then looked away. He'd then rush to a mirror. Anxiously, he asked his reflection in that shiny, silvery, magic frame:

"Mirror, mirror, on the wall, am I not
fairer than my son?"

He listened impatiently, but heard no response.
"Of course," he quickly chanted, "I am, I am,
I am."

He passed me by with a satisfied smirk:
"You're not so handsome, little squirt.
I remain the prince, the prince of this
domain. Ha!" He snapped his fingers
in my face. And when he did, I saw
the demon that possessed him.

I shivered with fear in my lonely crib.
My arms dared not reach out. Stuck
inside my shoulder sockets, they made
me look deformed.

"I'll get even with you, you distorted
bastard," I vowed with my soul's
unconscious vengeance—I felt like an
orphan. No one paid attention. I lay
drowning in my dirty diapers, the
stench pervading my entire body.

And then one day, my mother
suggested most delicately to my father,
"Don't you think you should bid your
son goodbye? After all, you won't be
home until late tonight. He needs a
father image to emulate. Otherwise,
he'll become too feminized."

My father roared with laughter. His son—ha ha—too feminized? "I'll go see the twerp. Let him idolize his father, a healthy, handsome specimen."

When our eyes met, my father recoiled in terror—from my soul came forth his reflected hatred. This shocked him to his core. He rushed to the mirror once again and renewed his former lie.

"He's a handsome boy," he stammered to my mother, feigning love and pride. "He'll keep you company while I'm working like a slave to keep the family out of poverty."

My mother felt much better at his fatherly concern, but a gnawing apprehension kept her awake at night. She shrugged it off, though, and went into my room where she diapered me and sang to me, whispering lovingly into my soul:

> You're mine, all mine,
> yum, yum.
> You give me joy, which he
> seldom does.
> Nobody else can have you,
> yum, yum.
> Mine, little Jesse, all mine!

Jesse was astonished at the insights that were emerging from his unconscious as he unfolded this tale. He was becoming aware of how much negative impact his father still had on his psyche, and at the same time a new perception was dawning about his relationship to his mother. He understood why he was more comfortable with her, who, beginning in childhood, treated him like her "little man." The demonic voices of both parents permeated Jesse's psyche.

I'm just no good. He doesn't want me. She does, but is her caring for me healthy? Jesse wondered.

> I'm her little man, I am.
> But why do I want to kill her—
> at age fifteen?
> She was on barbiturates, stumbling

around the house, her brassiere unhooked, her breasts exposed. She was showing me her crotch, which oozed with fluid, enough to make me vomit but heave with desire.

I approached her with an erection. Somehow she became conscious, pushed me away, and fled to her bedroom, while I remained in heat, almost demented from passion.

She doesn't want me either, my voices drummed into me. I ran to the kitchen and opened a drawer. A butcher knife was visible. I grabbed it, ready to use, then looked for my mother.

She was locked inside her room. I banged until my hands were bloodied. From the other side of the door came her rasping "Go away!"

Another rejection, another "not good enough!" My restraint vanished. I went berserk.

I plunged the knife into the wooden door, again and again, as though the knife were my phallus and the door her helpless crotch. I ejaculated copiously, which shocked me to the core.

I left the scene and ran into the streets, looking for an answer. No one was available—no one was around—to listen to this lost, desperate, young man.

I returned to the apartment: The door
was still locked, her snores resounding
through the walls. I pulled out the
knife, threw it back into the drawer,
went to my bedroom, and shouted:

"Whoever's up there…God? Explain
to me what just happened!" I heard
nothing. Yet I felt better.

From that moment on until her death, I
looked at her dispassionately—as
though she didn't exist. I became
aware of her repeated maneuvers to
touch me, excite me, and then push
me away. Her tactics were maddening.

No wonder I responded at fifteen in the
way that I did.

She was affected by drugs, but it was
her frustration with my father that had
untold power over her sense of self.
She'd become an empty shell, a robot
in a human form, mobilized by her
demons—who possessed her body,
mind, and soul.

"Mom," I cry silently, "why did you let
this happen? Didn't you have an ounce
of strength to fight against his
onslaught? God, spare me such a life.
Protect me from my father's tyranny."

"What an experience, Jesse," I commented. "I'm astonished that
you've held on to your sanity."

"She really played with me, dangling me like a little toy—all of it was her acting out because of her frustrated life with my father. I went through it in pain and anguish most of the time; but I never wanted her after that experience. I realized much later that I had been a breath away from being my mother's murderer and would have been convicted for life."

"How true, Jesse, a breath away," I sighed, feeling in awe of at the miraculous outcome.

After a pause, I said gently, "I'd like to talk about how this experience affected your relationship with women. But take some time first, so that what you've just worked through can be absorbed. We can pick it up next time."

As he walked out the door to leave, I hugged him gently and said, "Jesse, do you realize how brave you are and what excellent work you are doing here? You should feel very good about yourself."

CHAPTER 3

When Jesse arrived for our next appointment, I could see that his step was lighter and the tone of his skin was better. He looked happy to see me and readied himself for another hour of difficult work.

Raising the issue of our previous session, I asked, "How did what we talked about last time affect your relationship with women?"

Jesse explained, "They're not real to me. I use them for sex, but I'm afraid to love them, to really give myself to them. My father's attitude toward women didn't help either. His demonic intention runs around in my brain like a rat chasing a mouse:"

Father's Voice: The woman is to be seen and not heard from, and she should listen to what I say. Otherwise, I'll fuck around. So, pay attention to me, wife, and forget the kids.

Demonic Intention: What do you need a woman for? They'll drag you down. You don't need any ball-busting cunt to drain the life out of you. You want a career as an actor. If you listen to me, you'll have a career. If you need to get your rocks off from time to time, then jerk off, become a queer, or have sex with prostitutes, but never, never get yourself seriously involved with a woman.

Jesse's Reactions: I can't have good sex with a woman. I'm too scared she'll overwhelm me—maybe like my mother did. I've got to keep her at a distance. But, I want to be touched and held. Oh, fuck it, I'll jerk off—it's easier. Then I'll treat her like a nothing.

"Dr. Anneliese, this is how I feel about women. It's a sick, sick voice: domineering, hateful, and cruel. But that's my attitude toward the woman, even today."

"You've completely imbibed your father's infiltrated attitudes, Jesse. How could you have done otherwise? Your mother was pathological in her behavior toward you, and because you fought to keep her off you, your only example for interaction between man and woman was your father."

Jesse was delighted to hear some validation from me about his difficult life. He was so excited to be listened to that often he would interrupt my sentences, offering more insights, more examples, more secrets that he had hidden from himself. His secrets were being exposed and consequently purged, giving him a freedom he had never before experienced.

"I've never had normal sex with a woman, except once when I was nineteen. But, how normal was the girl really to have put up with this scene: At midnight I sneaked her into my bedroom in my parents' apartment. Not only were my parents in the next room, but my brother was sleeping on the other side of our shared room."

Jesse took a moment to reflect on what he was telling me. He shook his head in disbelief about his sense of unreality at that age. "What futility, what utter craziness," he exclaimed. "This shows you how out of it I was then. Nothing worked under such circumstances except to reinforce my fear of women. I had the right impulse, but I was so completely confused, I couldn't tell right from wrong."

"You've never loved any woman, Jesse?" I asked. "You've never consummated sexually with a so-called normal woman?"

"Only with call girls," Jesse answered sadly. He paused, started to speak again, and then turned his face away for a moment. When he turned back to me, his face lit up. "There's one woman I would have loved if I could love. I was with her while I still was working in films. Her name was Gabrielle, and she was working as a call girl. It was different with her. Everything worked between us, but then I got scared, overwhelmed, by my desire for her. I rejected her cruelly. I was convinced that giving in to the love I felt for her would have meant death."

Recalling his relationship with Gabrielle, Jesse had to stop speaking—tears were flowing from his eyes. He was embarrassed at how much feeling he had for her. After he wiped his eyes, he looked at me sorrowfully and asked, "When are the voices going to stop plaguing me?" His eyes were begging me to help him with his constant anguish. Suddenly he screamed out, "Death! Death is what it feels like to love a woman. I must be crazy!"

"You're in transition in your therapy, Jesse. Be patient with yourself. Remember that even a short time ago you would never have had the amount of consciousness to enable you to make such a statement.

"Jesse, go over to the bed. Beat the bed to vent your rage at the voices. That way they will lose their power."

> Get out of me, lump of a father. You
> disaster! You pig! Oh, how I loathe you
> and everything you stand for. But I'm
> not you, I'm me—Jesse. Maybe I'm a
> film star of the past—but I was a film
> star for a while. Natas took it all away.
> I succumbed to your evil, Natas, and to
> my father's. His and yours are the
> same.

"Good, Jesse," I chimed in. "You're realizing that the voices in both Natas and your father are satanic and evil. You invited them into your psyche because you were alone, lonely, a Not I in this world. You succumbed because you were so lost."

"So horribly lost, Dr. Anneliese. So horribly lost without a self. I listened like a needy, befuddled child. Now I'm stuck with these rattling, witchy voices that are drumming, pounding into my helpless brain: 'You're nothing, nothing, nobody—a piece of shit, kid. You're shit, you don't exist!' I could go mad from their incessant prattle," Jesse belted out, holding his hands on either side of his head.

"A profound truth, Jesse. Their purpose is to drive you mad. Some people, with less strength and awareness than you, have gone mad. Fight, Jesse, fight. In time you'll learn that they really are cowards and can be vanquished."

Jesse absorbed the words he had been shouting as well as mine. He dropped the racquet and sat at the edge of the bed. We sat in fertile silence.

I watched his complexion turn from a mottled red to a streaky yellow, and his bright blue eyes disappeared behind his eyelids into nowhere—an unfathomable nowhere—giving him the appearance of an empty-socketed corpse. I gave him time to sift through his feelings. As the minutes passed, I was witness to a brewing cyclone of an intensity that could destroy mountains. Jesse began muttering to himself with a growing consciousness:

> My father is demonic, like Natas. He's a
> conglomeration of all the evil that's
> ever existed in the world. To hate your
> own offspring so vehemently is an
> indescribable evil.

He became quiet as his realizations escalated into a monumental consciousness that could never be taken away from him. I waited until I saw him reach for the racquet. His skin returned to a scarlet hue while he hit the bed powerfully—with a strength enveloped by truths that would forever be seared into his psyche:

> You're rotten, Pop. Get out of me,
> along with Natas—along with anyone
> who stinks like you. Evil stinks because
> it comes from a hateful, breathless
> body and a heartless soul. I've been
> there—no more, no more! Take my
> vengeful feelings and die, Pop. You,
> too, Natas. I'm me: Joshua Jacobs;
> Jesse Jason; Jacobs—the son of an
> upholsterer from the Jewish ghetto of
> New York City. I'm all of it—me—me.
> The son of a tyrant father and a crazy
> mother.

Jesse kept mumbling to himself, "the son of a tyrant father and a crazy mother." He was trying to impress this truth upon his brain. The pivotal truth that finally dawned on him was that it was not his psyche that was distorted—but theirs. And their distortions were not his fault—they were generational.

Had Jesse not had enough awareness to probe his psyche for his true self, he too would have bequeathed the generational distortions to his future offspring.

Using the racquet to point into his parents' imaginary faces, he shouted his revelations at them:

> Wow. Wow! I finally get it! We're three
> different people. I'm a soul—different
> from him, different from her. I'm me, a
> Not I pushing toward being an I, and
> maybe even more. And that's the truth.

Jesse's enthusiasm could not be contained. I opened my mouth to say something, but closed it quickly because he shouted again, resembling an exploding star, throwing light everywhere.

> I'm not them, Dr. Anneliese, I'm me.
> I'm Jesse...Jesse.

Jesse left the session feeling like an autonomous three-year-old. He repeated like a mantra: "Jesse, Jesse, I'm Jesse..." He was still mumbling his name as he closed the office door.

Through my window, I watched him leave the office building and observed his feet stomping on the sidewalk to the rhythm of his name. He was not deterred by the passersby who perceived him to be slightly mad. When I observed the rest of his body, I noticed a broad smile broadcasting his pleasure. I watched Jesse's absorption with his name until he disappeared into a bus.

I, too, was smiling, as I returned to my desk, remembering the first recognition of my name and that that name was me; it was no one else's—mine. I was in tune with Jesse's monumental discovery and relished it completely. I wondered, too, what the next meeting would bring. Would Jesse be able to retain his good feelings?

CHAPTER 4

When we met again, Jesse was sitting in the waiting room, humming to himself. His humming scaled the high octaves. Joy filled the little waiting room as he hit his Jesse high notes. I led him into my office and suddenly his voice dropped to a tenor's voice, still mouthing: "Jesse. Jesse. I'm Jesse." His feet once again stomped to the rhythm of his name. He looked at me with amusement; it was clear that his last session was still reverberating in him and into this one.

"Well, little Jesse, how are you?" I asked.

"I'm afraid to stop singing for fear the darkness will take over and my identity will be taken away."

"Have you been singing all week long, then?" I asked bemused.

"Yup," he said. "All week long—and I love this little boy, my little Jesse."

"Why don't you hold little Jesse and tell him what you feel about him? Take this pillow and visualize it to be him. Can you do that?"

"I sure can," said Jesse as he took a beautiful green pillow from my bed and placed it on his lap. No time elapsed before the adult Jesse was healing the hurt, unloved infant. Jesse looked into the eyes of this imagined boy-child whom he held tenderly and sensitively. "You have blue eyes, little baby. Blue, blue eyes that sparkle even at such a young age. Can you smile for me? I'll tickle your chin, I'll kiss you all over so that you giggle. I'll lift you into the air and bring you back into my lap. There, there, you like that, and you're smiling, and you're looking at me as though you recognize me. I'm you and you are me, and I love you, precious baby."

I watched Jesse project his love into this infant's fragile, yearning system.

"This is so satisfying, Dr. A.," said Jesse after a while. "I could play with him all day long. I feel as though I'm being healed too. I would make a good father, wouldn't I?" he asked, looking to me for confirmation

"A loving and amazing father," I told him.

He took in my positive assessment of him, knowing that I would not lie. Heartened as we all are by someone else's good feelings toward us, he then imagined the infant growing into his adolescent self. Jesse hesitated for a moment, not wishing to recall this difficult phase of his life. Quickly, however, he manipulated the pillow so that it stood vertically in his lap, giving the imagined adolescent the size of a fifteen-year-old boy. He looked into the boy's eyes and told him, "You were never loved properly, Jesse. But I'll give you all the love in my heart. Feel my heart's warmth, bathe in it, soak in it so that you'll know someone is there for you. You never had that, did you? But you have it now, talented young boy who will no longer flounder by yourself. I'm going to hold you to my heart so that you'll feel my breath breathe with yours. You're of my flesh and I'll take care of you, school you, and nurture you like you've never been nurtured. You belong to me, growing Jesse, and you can ask for what you want. What you ask for will be granted." Jesse held the pillow to his body and suddenly burst into long-overdue, heart-wrenching sobs.

I wiped away my tears as I sat and empathized with the scene across from me. Jesse stayed with his young self for a long while, healing both of their wounds. He was exhausted and would have stopped had I not reminded him that there was another self waiting to be defined.

"Your adult self, Jesse. What about him?" With no hesitation, Jesse burst forth with the following soliloquy:

> You're a great guy—real, honest, and
> sensitive. I love you, handsome actor. I
> love your talent. Finally, I see and
> know you, and I love that you exist.
> You know what? You and I are going to
> do great films from now on. Films with

meaning and beauty. I'm going to be
proud of them. What do you think of
that?

Jesse's eyes sparkled. He returned to his seat and wiped his face with
a tissue. When I felt he was ready, I asked him to define his me more
clearly—his I.

He didn't hesitate for a moment. He bubbled forth:

> I have integrity. I didn't always, but I
> got a whiff of what integrity feels like
> when I defied Natas for the first time at
> the beginning of our contact.

> I'm creative, loving, joyful. I'm sexy
> and I love being inside a woman. I
> know I'm not "queer"—to use my
> demonic father's term for gays.

> I love my work as an actor. I've got to
> get back to it, but first things first. I
> have to straighten myself out. I've got
> more voices to tackle. A major one has
> to do with my work. My father wanted
> to be sure I wouldn't be successful, and
> I have to acknowledge that Natas was
> instrumental in my getting work. But
> once I was in films, I got acclaim on
> my own.

Jesse hadn't been addressing me directly; it was more as though
he were talking to himself. Just then, he looked in my direction, and I
could sense that more layers of Jesse's psyche needed to be exposed and
expressed.

"What is it, Jesse?"

"Dr. A., even though my father has been dead for many years, his voice drums on and on in me. As soon as I feel the good part of me, I can hear that ugly tone of his."

"What is he saying?"

Father's Voice: I can't believe you're up for a part in a soap. I didn't get what I wanted. Why should you? You're getting more than I did.

Demonic Intention: You won't get that part. If you do, be shitty and cruel. They won't give it to you, though. You're too honest. You make me wanna puke. You'll get the shaft if you're too honest. Listen to me; I know how it is out there…

Jesse's Reactions: I'm not good enough to get anything. But, wait a minute, I must have talent; otherwise they wouldn't have chosen me. Oh, I'm so mixed up. It was Natas who got the jobs for me; I couldn't have gotten them by myself. I'm not worth a producer's time. But, the producers did choose me…I'm handsome, but not as handsome as my father. Look at my arms, anyone can see I'm deformed…What would I do without Natas? And what's wrong with being honest? Oh, I'm so mixed up.

Jesse buried his face in his hands. "Dr. Anneliese, did you hear what I just said? I've already lost all the realizations, insights, and good feelings I had before—they disappeared. Just a simple recall of my father's demonic attack makes me instantly feel as though I'm being buried alive by volcanic lava. In a split second, I become obliterated and crawl back into a Not I hole."

"It's okay, Jesse. It's like that sometimes. Just keep exploring what's there, and you'll find your I again."

Jesse sighed, but he picked up his head and continued:

"I remember when I was a kid…I would pick up the phone, and my pop would be on the other end. He'd just breathe into the phone, and I was sent into a Not I state: I'd get confused and couldn't talk straight. I'd stutter, which gave him more reasons to belittle me. When the call was finished, I'd sit on my bed and perspire as though I'd been in a boxing ring. He was wearing the boxing gloves, though, not me. Sometimes it took a whole week to shake off his voices. His voices were my ego, and I functioned from them—big time. When I was older, I'd booze the voices away. I'd get sick as a dog and vomit, but somehow I'd eventually get back to my usual unbalanced self, the Jesse I was then."

"As a result of all the work you've been doing on yourself, Jesse, I would say that you have a good understanding of how the voices work. Without your consciousness, they would take over as they did in your life before therapy. We human beings vacillate in our warriorship against the evil forces. But do know that pursuing your battle with them eventually will eradicate them—and the boxing gloves will adorn your hands, not Satan's.

"Now that you have become more cognizant, can you imagine still being susceptible to a Natas, who a few years ago told you,

> He's ripe for my domain. I won't even
> need a blood bond for him to fuse with
> me. He's so ready, so willing—so lost.

"Never!" Jesse yelled emphatically. After a few seconds, he said, *"I hope never."*

CHAPTER 5

Over the next three years, Jesse worked diligently to gain an I. He realized he must do so to stave off the satanic energy that feeds on those who are lost to themselves.

While working as an actor, Jesse had been in a Not I state—open to satanic infiltration—and had succeeded in the film industry through a blood bond with Natas. He'd sold out. In time, his psyche deteriorated, his career collapsed, and he hit bottom.

Nonetheless, his soul awakened, as most souls do if this esoteric organ retains within itself a modicum of God's energy and design. He told me about his career, from its height to its ultimate demise:

> I got rid of Gabrielle...Too much
> synchronicity tapping into my heart
> and all its desire—"Out you go, whore.
> You're responsible for my flaccid penis.
> I'll hire another cunt to prove I'm
> potent."
>
> I went to the studio and strutted like a
> sultan, an unaware replication of my
> father, behaving from demonic
> motivation.
>
> The African movie had repercussions.
> My producer, Frank, investigated what
> Rang-Ta really meant. From that

moment on, he looked at me as though
I were the devil, and clearly he
believed that Kuwa—the hired extra
from the African village—had spoken
the truth.

I blurted foul language around the cast.
My sensibilities were distorted—
infiltrated, I would say. Frank judged
every move I made.

Unfortunately, as I became less
revered by him and the cast my
demonic ego craved their respect ever
more desperately. I floundered,
stuttered in fear, and exposed a
vulnerability that was embarrassing to
behold. In time, Frank became
impatient with my radical changes of
mood.

He told the others I was crazy and
hopelessly possessed. The backers
believed him and fired me on the spot.
They finished the film without my help,
but it was put on the shelf.

I screamed for Natas to help me, but
many months passed before the
creature showed its face. Meanwhile
my reputation suffered—"disintegrated"
is a truer word. No one wanted to hire
me for another film; they called me
Rang-Ta and spat upon me as an evil
force.

I tried to explain, but my lips refused

to articulate that it wasn't I who was
the devil—but that it was Natas who
had become my other self.

"I'm not Natas," I sobbed pitifully,
silently, falling on the ground. I slid
along the earth on my belly, like a
lowly, cursed reptile.

The warm earth granted me support.
"Mom," I whispered, burrowing my face
as though I'd returned into her
comforting womb, "you're here—don't
go away, I can't do without you."
Suddenly I recognized what I was
doing. "Jesse, get up," said a healthier
part of me.

I rose from the ground and went on my
way—bewildered, lost, and desperate.
There was nothing I could do; they'd
made their decision. No one came forth
with sympathy. At that moment, reality
struck me: Fame is meaningless.
Humanity's Not I is not dissimilar to
mine.

Natas finally appeared, but arrogant
and cruel, ordering me to bow to it. I did, but I
questioned It, "Why this
denigration?"

"No reason, Jesse," It replied
nonchalantly. "I want to be upheld by
you as a god, instead of getting your
repulsion."

"You've helped me a lot, and for that
I'm truly grateful. But why do you wish
to destroy me now when my entire life
is crumbling?"

"No reason, Jesse. It's just my whim.
I'm tired of supporting you. Besides,
there are more qualified souls waiting
anxiously to join me. You've been on
the fence as long as I've known you.
"Total submission is the key to my
return. So long, Jesse, we've had a
good connection. I'm overworked;
you're one less soul to tend to. You've
fared well for many years. Now fend for
yourself. If in time you need my help
again, you'll have to beg me for my
presence."

I stood on my feet, totally destroyed,
but I mobilized my feelings and thrust
my tightly clenched fists into the air
where Natas had stood sneering. I
punched and punched, shouting, "You
lousy bastard, rot in your hell. Who
needs your crocodilian handouts? I'd
rather die!"

"You do, Jesse!" Natas replied,
reappearing and grinding its teeth.
"You hate me," it snorted, "always
have. I put up with you because you
had potential: a lost soul, sometimes a
willing sheep. Let's see how you
survive without my assistance. Call on
me when you're really distraught and
you appreciate my handouts—ha ha—

as gifts from a god."

With that response, Natas disappeared. I looked around and found myself sitting in the street—homeless, in shabby clothes, with slippers on my feet and a sign asking for help. Gabrielle's earrings kept me from starvation but not from my personal anguish.

I tried drugs and alcohol, but none of them worked. I knew it was time to face myself.

Nevertheless…

Two years passed in this desolation: I slept on the streets, a drugged Not I blinded by its own degradation. My soul ached from my abuse, but I couldn't stop myself from its obsessive momentum.

One dark day, I heard Natas' ranting filling the atmosphere. I trembled with fear, mixed with desire, to plead for its gifts—to be given its recompense in return for my soul.

Natas approached me, sneering. "You're still on the streets, Jesse. A nothing, a nobody, a piece of shit. Nothing but a lost boy." It took a breath and then continued ranting, while I became its totally bedeviled audience.

"You had it good for a long, long time, Jesse: money, fame, classy prostitutes. All of that is yours—just say the word. Submission is a meager price to pay for such generous rewards. You know it's much easier with my help, son of a lowly upholsterer. You can't do it by yourself.

"Here's my syringe—let's bond a second time. But this time it's for good. Forever. Uh-huh, ha ha! You'll be mine for keeps, yum yum. For eternity."

My heart pounded frightfully as Natas approached. I said, "But I don't understand. You disposed of me a while ago."

"I did, didn't I, but I was too harsh. I'm willing to give you another chance. I'll help you turn Frank's crazy decision around, and the film will be released. The world will see it and give you rave reviews. Your fame will be reestablished."

 "You can do all that?" I asked, like a child in wonder, still wanting acceptance from my poppa. I visualized my name on a theater canopy:

JESSE JASON in AFRICAN STORY

Once again, I was mesmerized by the fantasy of a life of glamour, interviews,

and star-crazed women at my feet. The
dream overtook me while Natas
chanted, "You're a piece of shit without
me; you need my voice to guide you."

Natas' needle was poised and ready to
pierce my delicate vein. But,
suddenly—as though I were being
struck by lightning darting through
from another sphere into my brain and
heart—I remembered Gabrielle: her
warmth, her caring, and her beauty. I
remembered the love we shared, if
only for a few moments."

Then I recalled my forlorn self—a
resigned, fearful little boy who let
myself be bullied by my father, as well
as by others in my life.

Revolted by this passive self, I
underwent a major shift. Instead of
surrendering to Natas' power, I feinted
and parried with Its syringe: dodging
here and there, up and down, and
circling it as well. In confusion, Natas
grunted and hissed, but my human
body was too swift for its reptilian
weight and narcissistic cunning. I took
a deep breath, mustering gargantuan
strength.

In doing so, I became the real Jesse
Jacobs—battling with the giant Goliath.
I shouted so loud the mountaintops
broke into a million pieces crashing to
the earth. "Don't come near me, you

disgusting monster. Don't come near
me ever again. I don't want you, I
want me! I'll do it for myself."

I repeated these commands, again and
again, until no breath was left.

Natas disappeared, with grunting,
hissing, snorting, fire-belching sounds.
It was talking to itself, sniveling that it
had lost a soul.

❧

Jesse stood before me looking huge, muscular, and confident. He
remained silent for a long time. I let him stay this way. I realized that he
was changing a lifetime pattern of terror and cowardice and acquiring
a new, assertive self. Such a change is a major feat in a person's psyche;
the old way of being needs to be discarded and sensitively replaced with
new feelings—feelings with which we are all endowed from birth but
that all too soon are tampered with by an evil environment.

When I looked at him again, it seemed that he was readier to
continue. I asked him, "Who are you, Jesse?" At first, he didn't hear
me, so ensconced was he in the impressive character he was portraying.
Finally he told me that he was David of the Old Testament—not little
David who fought the giant, but big David, God's beloved. He had
learned about big David in Hebrew School as a child and always felt a
kinship with him.

"There's nothing I can't do," he boasted, gesticulating into the air as
though he owned it. "David lived in God's favor, but in time he betrayed
God's covenant. I've been there, too, haven't I, with Natas? But I'm no
longer in that place."

"Where are you, David?" I asked, making the error of not calling
him Jesse because his new self was so convincing. At this, Jesse laughed
uproariously. He seemed to be on stage with his portrayal of strength,
and that the audience was totally with him. "Oh, Dr. A., the Not I that
I have been living from was sin in its utmost hell. I never want to fall

back. I've broken out of a gigantic, encrusted, evil shell that kept me hidden from my I."

"Are you in your I now, Jesse?" I asked.

"I believe so. I feel so. I know so," he told me, wanting a small degree of affirmation from me. I gave it to him.

"It is so, Jesse—and more."

"It is so, and more," he repeated. "More...he repeated again, quizzically. "You're right. Do you know what else I feel? And this feeling is new. I have the image of a pregnant woman. As her womb gets accustomed to the new life inside her, she also has the impression there's another life growing beside the one that's there. I feel like that; there's another I—bigger, grander, stronger, wiser, all encompassing—growing alongside the other I."

Jesse touched his belly, then his heart, then his forehead. He breathed into his body strongly and fully. "It's big, this other thing. In contrast, my little ego seems so picayune, so insignificant, so incidental. Yet it's necessary; I need it in this world." He was silent again, trying to fathom what he was intuiting.

"Might you be giving birth to your I Am, Jesse?" I asked when I thought he was ready for another question.

"Me? Me, Dr. A.?"

"You! Why not you? Do you want God in your life?"

He sat in deep thought. He knew it was a huge question and he did not wish to answer superficially. I waited as Jesse tapped into the well of his own life force, which had been unthawing for the past five years. He dipped down deeply to his heart's core and his soul, asking for answers to my question.

After a long while, in what is known as a stage whisper—which simulates a modulated tone of voice but can be heard by the last row in a theater—he whispered clearly and forcefully: "I want God. I've been with you, Satan. I want God! Do you hear me, Satan? I want God! Remember how you punished me because I called on God? Well, I don't care what you do to me now, because I'm strong, like David, and I can stick to my convictions without being scared of you, Pop; of you, Satan; of anyone in this world, because I'm Jesse, Jesse, no longer the son of a Jewish upholsterer, but the son—the child—of God. That's who I am!

That's who I was when I came into my mother's womb, and that's who I'm becoming again: Jesse, the creation of God!"

"Jesse, you said it. I believe you."

"You bet I said it. And I mean it!"

My eyes teared. How exquisite the human soul becomes when it surpasses the Not I and I and reaches for the I Am, I thought to myself. I embraced Jesse, who stood before me like a hungry boy, finally feeling understood, appreciated and cared for.

He broke down and fell to his knees, embracing the lower half of my body like a five-year-old boy embracing his mother. I lowered myself to the floor next to him and pulled him into my lap. I cradled him and gave him my loving energy. He sobbed deeply and, for the moment at least, his tears—long repressed, ancient tears—washed away his pain. A moment like this added to other moments in time engenders a healing.

I sang to him, too. Where the words came from I do not know—I would guess from my heart and soul:

> Jesse, Jesse, a valiant soul,
> shipwrecked and drowning. I rock you
> to bring God's comfort to a love-
> starved boy whose heart needs
> healing. Touch your true nature,
> devised by your Maker. Meet it,
> connect to it—your true Self,
> your I Am.
>
> This ultimate master will guide you
> with wisdom, love, and with power.
>
> Shout your desires to the great
> Mightiness. Soar like an eagle to the
> rim of his heaven. Shout to him, now,
> Jesse, and confide in him your desires.

Jesse reluctantly let go of my body and propelled himself forward into kneeling. Looking toward the heavens, he spoke plainly, simply, humbly:

> Let me in.
> It's time,
> my loving Father.

He shyly returned to my lap, snuggling closer and closer into my body. He was overcome with uplifting joy throughout my invocation to his soul and during his effort to speak to the Lord.

We both waited for a response. When none came, Jesse, his head resting on my shoulder, cried softly and mumbled pitifully, "Why should you, Lord? Why should you respond to me? I'm nothing, a nobod—"

His victimized thought was interrupted by a whisper in the room—a sweet whisper, like a soft wind embracing our ears and hearts. The Lord said:

> *Stand tall, Jesse,*
> *my beautiful child.*
> *I rejoice at your transformation.*
> *I welcome you, my son.*

Jesse listened and heard, his mouth open in utter amazement. He looked toward me for confirmation that God was actually speaking to him, and that he, Jesse Jacobs, was worthy of such a gift. I just nodded, and the tears streamed down his face.

When we no longer heard the Lord's voice, Jesse leapt up from my lap all at once. Falling to his knees near the place where the voice had originated, he whispered hoarsely, and with gratitude:

> Thank you, God.

> AMEN.

I added:

So be it, Lord,
From now on,
and into eternity!

Epilogue

Gabrielle and Jesse are on their way. They are human beings on a journey from being a Not I to becoming an I, to reaching an I Am state—a state in partnership with God and his ways, where one listens only to the voice of God.

By the end of five years in therapy, each had grown an I and were approaching their I Am. They had had a taste, a memorable taste, of God in their lives as a result of their therapeutic unraveling. The seed of his love was in them, instilled by the Divinity from the time they were created. Finally they could recognize and be grateful for that seed, but it would need their nurturing on a daily basis.

Consciousness about the evil forces reached a high level for both of them as well. Had they not lived through Satan's pervasive infiltration throughout their lives? Their experiences taught them to be vigilant about such a mesmerizing and sinister force and to realize how fortunate they were to have gained awareness of Diablo's existence in their psyches.

Uppermost in their consciousness, however, had been implanted the desire to speak with God, their first love—and the knowing that he would respond. This desire needed to be strengthened and revitalized as often as breathing—through prayer; by knocking on God's door and expecting the door to be opened; and whenever they asked, by trusting that they would be heard and given to.

They both knew they had more work to do to reach the level of trust that could never be shaken by any outer circumstance. They were willing, however—even eager—to press on, to remain so open to God that his voice would always be the dominant voice in their lives.

Gabrielle had taken the huge step of forgiveness. It was now her task to sustain her faith and the willingness to make her wholeness the most vital aspiration of her life.

Although Jesse had not yet forgiven his parents, he realized that to sustain his newly found I Am, he would need to tend to this unfinished business. He knew that forgiveness was a necessary step for true rebirth of his psyche. He also knew that by forgiving his parents, he could leave them behind so that they, too, could move ahead with their lives.

Jesse even looked forward to forgiving them, but he wanted to deeply feel that step, not merely mouth it. He did not wish to be either a Judas Iscariot, who crucified his Christed self, or a St. Peter, who betrayed his Christed self.

Anyone who has lived through satanic infiltration and desires to eradicate it has had to struggle with it on a daily basis, as we know St. Paul did. With that wakefulness, we are on our way to a greater Self. We are on the path to that grander Self when we apply ourselves to a monumental truth spoken by Jesus:

> *If we do not bring forth what is within us, what we do not bring forth will destroy us. But, if we bring forth what is within us, what we bring forth will save us.* [17]

Such is our journey in life. And the greatest passion in our hearts is our love for and communion with God.

Jesse and Gabrielle wanted all of it.

THE END

Gabrielle sat in my waiting room. A blond, male patient entered and sat opposite her, holding a container in his hand filled with a hot liquid. She commented, "That smells like hot chocolate."

"It is," he told her, observing her dark, beautiful features. "Can I share some with you?"

"I'd love that," she replied, handing him her empty container.

They looked at each other intently now. "Jesse?" Gabrielle asked, as she scrutinized his face.

"Gabrielle?" Jesse questioned delicately. Repressing his deep excitement, he poured hot chocolate into her container.

"I have a lemon tart I'd like to share," she told him.

"Great."

They sat silently, eyes averted, drinking the hot chocolate and eating the lemon tart. As they did so, the past trickled through their bodies like polluted water loaded with satanic inheritances, which felt like ugly worms creeping out from every crevice in their bodies and psyches. Gabrielle jerked her body involuntarily as though she were pushing them away. Jesse's body gyrated forcefully, wanting to shake them off into the earth, into which they could burrow and disappear forever.

The transmutation was brief. They then slipped back into savoring their drink and pastry with the same mesmerized pleasure a child derives from its mother's breast.

Jesse became aware of a deep sorrow in him. His heart told him, you've hurt this woman. Make amends. But he lacked the courage. Instead, he silently asked Gabrielle for forgiveness. As his thought entered Gabrielle's consciousness, she instinctively turned her head to the right, pushing away his desire.

Jesse, recalling his newfound David strength, was not deterred. He tried again, out loud this time. "Forgive me. I was so unconscious." She turned her head to the other side—no one would ever misuse her again!

"Forgive me, beautiful Gabrielle," he pleaded from his heart. Her whole body remained guarded against his words; but a feeling surged though Jesse's entire being, a love that was pure and simple, a love he had never experienced before. At that moment, Gabrielle reacted to these feelings. Slowly, she shifted her gaze toward him and rested it on his face. She said nothing, but after a short while their blue, blue eyes intermingled. A tiny smile grew on her lips. He smiled back gratefully.

As they were finishing their shared repast, it occurred to both of them that they each had been visiting Dr. Anneliese's office unbeknownst to the other. They had never met there before.

When I encountered Gabrielle and Jesse sitting in my waiting room, I was shocked. I thought that a mistake in scheduling had been made.

Was it mine? I wondered, or was it God's timing? When my shock had subsided, I answered my own question, silently, smiling at them from God's love: It doesn't matter. It just is!

AFTERWORD

This book has been in the making ever since I discovered the reality of the parental demonic infiltration (and in later years, satanic infiltration) into the psyche. When one of my editors suggested that I write an Afterword, I realized that I could do so because I am still involved with the topic, both personally and professionally, on an almost daily basis. I didn't wish to have this involvement, but the persistent satanic nudges, interferences—some of them dangerous—put a wedge into my life, and I knew I could not move forward until I faced those voices and destroyed them like the moving figures in a shooting gallery at a carnival.

Out of nowhere, whether I am by myself or with others, even now the voice can loom forth at any time. When I am alone, I can readily tell it to disappear, to "get behind me, Satan." When in the company of others, however, this is not so easily done—unless you have exceptional friends who will not think you strange when you abruptly stop your conversation with them, turn to an invisible enemy, and physically and vocally tell IT to go back to hell.

The struggles that Gabrielle and Jesse faced, the struggles I have faced, exist for most of us—in different forms, depending on the circumstances of our lives. Are not these experiences akin to facing the dark night of the soul, to walking through the dark night of the spirit?

You, the reader, may have fallen at any point into agonizing trials resulting in depression, anger, fear, hatred, frustration—any or all of these human feelings. It is at such a time that vigilance about the enticing dark forces must be kept uppermost in your psyches. It is the time of the dark night of the soul, which, creates a Not I state, causing you to wander, lost in the unlit labyrinth, wondering where you are going, who you are, and asking why you are living this dismal existence.

These are the times when the dark night of the spirit is in ascendancy—no God to implore…no angels…no heaven…no faith in anything…no soul to prompt you. You feel as though you exist, hanging haphazardly off of an isolated star in one of the constellations.

If only we were aware. If only we had the consciousness to understand that releasing ourselves from the satanic forces in any form is our first mission in this life. This need to be fully conscious of this entity's existence in our lives—in all of our lives, even if we have reached the highest spiritual levels—is critically important. And we must ask for the courage to risk our life, if that is necessary, in order to get free.

The purpose of this book has been to show the reader how to return to the Source, devoid of the evil ones. My aim was to bring to the reader ways to master these forces and to remember the origin we all share—our Source, the vital life force of our true self—and to ally with it. It is our friend and guide. It is available to all who seek it.

Jesus, who knew his destiny and who had to overcome its horrendous trials, can serve as a wayshower to those who want to look toward him as such. We too have trials—our trials to achieve consciousness so that we can become aware of the invading forces, fight them, struggle with our hardened heart, which ages ago separated itself from the Source.

Happily, the light of our consciousness, no matter how dimly or brightly illuminated, destines us to come back into union with that Source. The endless reasons we can give for our separation will reveal themselves to be illusory when we finally awaken to our true nature. When we have finally walked through the dark night of the soul—as well as the dark night of the spirit—and we are allied with our shiny new now-consciousness, we can be led out of the unlit labyrinth. We can say in a simple but heartfelt way to our Father—as Jesse and Gabrielle and many of my other patients have been able to do—

> "God, help me.
> I want to be one with you.
> I am yours! Not Its!"

End Notes

1. Marshall, Catherine, Beyond Our Selves, Baker Book House Company, Grand Rapids, MI, 1961, p. 152.

2. 1997, Available from Cypress House, (707) 964-9520.

3. The Common Rule—Dead Sea Scrolls, p. 237.

4. Paraphrased from Prophet, Elizabeth Clare, Forbidden Mysteries of Enoch, Fallen Angels and the Origins of Evil, Summit University Press, St. Louis, MO, 1983, pp. 8-14.

5. 1998, Available from Cypress House, (707) 964-9520.

6. Peck, Scott M., M.D., People of the Lie, a Touchstone Book, New York, NY, 1983, p. 82.

7. Peck, Scott M., M.D. Ibid, p. 82.

8. Oesterreich, T. K., Possession, Demoniacal & Other, Among Primitive Races in Antiquity, the Middle Ages, and Modern Times, University Books, New Hyde Park, NY, 1966, p. 7.

9. Pierrakos, John, M.D., The Energy Field in Man and Nature (Monograph), INAM, 1971, p. 10.

10. Pierrakos, John, M.D., Ibid, p. 14.

11. Pierrakos, John, M.D., The Core of Man (Monograph), INAM, 1974, p. 8.

12. Pierrakos, John, M.D., The Energy Field in Man and Nature (Monograph), INAM, 1971, p. 14.

13. Peck, M. Scott, M.D., Glimpses of the Devil, Free Press, New York, NY, 2005, p. 238.

14. 1997, Available from Cypress House, 800-773-7782.

15. The Holy Bible, Matthew 6:15.

16. Cruz, Nicky, with Frank Martin, Soul Obsession, Water Brook Press, Colorado Springs, CO, 2005, p. 95.

17. Miller, Robert J., The Complete Gospels, Harper, San Francisco, 1992, p. 316.

BIBLIOGRAPHY

1. Anderson, Neil T, Victory Over the Darkness, Regal Books, Ventura, CA, 1990.

2. Baldwin, William J., D.D.S., Ph.D., Spirit Releasement Therapy, Human Potential Foundation Press, 1992.

3. Baldwin, William J., Ph.D., Healing Lost Souls, Releasing Unwanted Spirits from Your Energy Body, Hampton Roads Publishing Company, Inc., 2003.

4. Cruz, Nicky with Frank Martin, One Holy Fire, Waterbrook Press, CO, 1973.

5. Cruz, Nicky with Frank Martin, Soul Obsession, Waterbrook Press, CO, 1973.

6. Cruz, Nicky, with Jamie Buckingham, Run Baby Run. Bridge-Logos Publishers, FL, 1968.

7. Freud, Sigmund, Studies in Parapsychology, A Neurosis of Demoniacal Possession in the Seventeenth Century, Collier Books, NY, 1971.

8. Freud, Sigmund, The Ego and the Id, translated by Joan Riviere, Revised and newly edited by James Strachey, The Norton Library, NY, 1960.

9. Frey-Rohn, Liliane, The Psychological View--Evil.

10. Hammond, Frank and Ida Mae, Pigs in the Parlor, A Practical Guide to Deliverance, Impact Books, Inc., Kirkwood, Mo., 1973.

11. Hannah, Barbara, Ego and Shadow, The Guild of Pastoral Psychology, Guild Lecture 85, March, 1955.

12. Lowen, Alexander, M. D., Physical Dynamics of Character Structure, Gruen & Stratton, NY, 1958.

13. Lowen, Alexander, The Betrayal of the Body, The Macmillan Co., 1967.

14. Malachi, Martin, Hostage to the Devil, Harper, San Francisco, 1976.

15. Marshall, Catherine, Beyond Our Selves, Chosen Books, Grand Rapids, Michigan, 1961.

16. Meurois-Givaudan, Anne and Daniel, The Ways of the Essenes, Christ's Hidden Life Remembered, Destiny Books, Rochester, Vermont, 1993.

17. Miller, Robert, J. The Complete Gospels, Harper, San Francisco, 1992.

18. Murphy, Ed, Dr., The Handbook for Spiritual Warfare, Thomas

19. Nelson Publishers, Nashville, Tennessee, 1992.

20. Ouspensky, P. D., Talks with a Devil, Samuel Weiser, Inc., York Beach, Maine, 1972.

21. Pagels Elaine, The Gnostic Gospels, Vintage Books, NY, 1979.

22. Pagels, Elaine, Adam, Eve and the Serpent, Vintage Books, NY, 1988.

23. Pagels, Elaine, Beyond Belief, Random House, NY, 2005.

24. Pagels, Elaine, The Origin of Satan, Random House, NY, 1995.

25. Peck, M. Scott, M. D. People of the Lie, the Hope for Healing Human Evil, A Touchstone Book, NY, 1983.

26. Peck, M. Scott, M. D., Glimpses of the Devil, Free Press, NY, London, Toronto, Sydney, 2005.

27. Peck, M. Scott, M. D., The Road Less Traveled, A Touchstone Book, NY, 1978.

28. Pierrakos, John, M. D., The Energy Field in Man and Nature (Monograph, INAM, 1971.

29. Pierrakos, John, The Core of Man (Monograph), INAM, 1974.

30. Prophet, Elizabeth Clare, Forbidden Mysteries of Enoch, Fallen Angels and the Origins of Evil, Summit University Press, Corwin Springs, MT, 1983.

31. Prophet, Elizabeth Clare, with Patricia R. Spadaro and Murray L. Steinman, Kabbalah, Key to Your Inner Power, Summit Press, Lexington, MT.

32. Prophet, Mark L., Elizabeth Clare, Climb the Highest Mountain, Book One, The Path of the Higher Self, Summit University Press, 1972.

33. Reich, Wilhelm, M.D., Reich Speaks of Freud, edited by Mary Higgins nd Chester Raphael, M. D., Farrar, Straus and Giroux, NY 1967.

34. Russell, Jeffrey Burton, The Devil, Perception of Evil from Antiquity to Primitive Christianity, Ithaca and London, 1977.

35. Sanford, John A., Evil, the Shadow Side of Reality, Crossroad, NY, 1994.

36. Sanford, John A., Jung and the Problem of Evil, The Strange Trial of Mr. Hyde, Sigo Press, Boston, 1987.

37. Sanford, John A., The Kingdom Within, The Inner Meaning of Jesus' Sayings, Harper, San Francisco, 1970.

38. Swedenborg, Emanuel, Conversations with Angels, Edited by Leonard Fox and Donald L. Rose, translated by David Gladish and Jonathan Rere, Chrysalis Books, West Chester, PA, 1996.

39. Swedenborg, Emanuel, Conversations with the Devil, 1996.

40. The Urantia Books, A Revelation, Uversa Press, NY, 2003.

41. Wangerin, Walter, Jr., The Book of the Dun Cow, Harper San Francisco, 1978.

Printed in the United States
216706BV00002B/1/P